Raw Revelation

The Bible They Never Tell You About

Mark Roncace

ISBN: 1479214183
ISBN 13: 9781479214181

Printed by CreateSpace, North Charleston, SC

To Rachel and Zachary

Man does not live by bread alone, but on every word that proceeds from the mouth of God.

Your words were found, and I ate them.

Table of Contents

INTRODUCTION

I should probably start with some sort of story to catch your attention. I could begin with an entertaining narrative about me as a little boy in Sunday school, or an account of an experience I had in Bible class in junior high or in those wonderful weekly chapel services in the un-air-conditioned gymnasium (in Florida). I could perhaps hook you with reflections about how my mother's faithful work with families of medically fragile children shaped and molded me. Or I could relate the unlikely sequence of events that landed me in the Introduction to Bible class in college that would change everything. Or a funny anecdote about how a devout nonbeliever — who just happened to be a pretty girl in my apartment complex in graduate school — prompted me to ponder some of life's big questions. I could tell about my work as a professor and some of the compelling interactions I have had with young people who are on journeys of their own. A cute story about the theological questions my little daughter or son has asked me, and how I muddled through a completely inadequate response, might do the trick.

But I won't begin that way. I can't. First impressions are crucial, and I want to make the right one. This book is not about me. It's about the Bible. This book is not about entertaining stories like the ones preachers tell to prevent us from nodding off. It's about dealing with hard truths. It's about being straight up and honest with ourselves, each other, and the Word of God. Thus, I want to be candid and forthright from the beginning.

It's the same with my students. On the first day of class, I consciously set the right tone for the whole term. I don't want to give them the idea that I will entertain, that they will sit passively and watch as I perform. So I don't start with some song and dance — it's not going to be like watching primetime on Fox. Nor do I want to convey the sense that it will be a boring class filled with long, dry lectures. Thus, I avoid commencing with the predictable distribution of the syllabus followed by a review of its even more predictable contents.

Rather, the impression I hope to give is that it will be a stimulating and engaging course. It's also going to be a lot of hard mental work. It's going to be a challenge. To that end, I walk in on the first day and immediately distribute a copy of Genesis 38 or Judges 19 or Song of Songs 5 with the verse numbers and other tell-tale markings eliminated. (Go ahead and take a peek at those texts and you'll see why I use them. Yes, I am pandering to my students' interest in sex and violence, but come on, *coitus interruptus* or the maiden declaring, "I had taken off my robe" and "my fingers dripped with liquid myrrh on the handle of the bolt" is far better than "Hi, welcome to our class.") Students read the text and then I pose a series of questions; they write their responses before sharing their thoughts with a partner. This initial exercise sets the table in the same way that I'd like to do so for you, the reader. There are three main points: (1) the Bible is full of fascinating and sometimes downright disturbing stuff which we don't hear much about; (2) we must read carefully, ask good questions, and think for ourselves; and (3) conversing with others should be an important part of the process.

The ultimate purpose of this book, then, is to encourage you to read another book, the Bible, in its entirety. Okay, maybe not the whole Bible, but good portions of it—at least more than the famous passages or favorite verses that we already know. So, if you have limited time (and who doesn't?), put down this book and find a Bible. The last thing this world needs is another commentary about the Bible when hardly anyone reads the Scripture itself. Seriously, go ahead and close this book and pick up a Bible. If you peruse not one more word of this book and instead study the Scripture for yourself and think openly and honestly about it, I will have succeeded. Conversely, if you read only this book and trust what I say, I will have failed miserably. If you intend to continue with this book, please locate a Bible to follow along as we explore the unfiltered, uncensored Word of God. Really, please, go find a Bible. Any translation will do—even *The Message*. There are a ton of Bibles online, so you can get them on your phone in which case it's like getting one long, long text message directly from God. And God doesn't like it when his texts are censored.

COOKING THE GOOD BOOK

The raw Bible is just too hard to swallow, or at least that is what preachers think. So they cook the Good Book. They butter it up and water it down to suit our tastes. They distill the Scripture, filtering out the unsightly and unpalatable passages. Just as processed and packaged foods are barely reminiscent of what first comes out of the ground or from the animal (think mac and cheese or hot dogs), so too the clean, attractive Bible that they present in church is a far cry from the real thing. Like parents who don't feed their children peas and carrots because they fear the kids won't like the vegetables, or worse, won't like mom and dad, so too preachers give us, the children of God, a candy and cookie Scripture because they want us to be happy and them to be liked. Consequently we aren't properly nourished. The body of Christ, the Church, has been deprived of the nutrition necessary to grow and develop healthily. But enough is enough. It's time for us to be fed the organic, all natural Bible. It's time for all of us to know the truth, the whole truth, about what's in our Scripture. We need God's raw Revelation.

Generally speaking, priests and pastors are good, caring, and honorable — generally speaking. Their job, in part, is to minister to people spiritually, emotionally, and materially, to encourage, inspire, support, and love the members of their congregations. Most clergy carry out these tasks with diligence and integrity. There is certainly more to being a preacher than preaching the Bible. Nevertheless, helping people to read, study, and understand the Scripture should be a significant part of the work of a responsible Christian leader. Likewise, there is more to being a Christian than knowing the Bible, but, still, knowledge of the Word should be one aspect of a deep, meaningful life of faith.

Make no mistake about it, raw Revelation is tough stuff — it's not tender and juicy. Preachers know how hard it is. They know what the Bible says. They know the truth. But, for them, it's just as well that we don't. They select short passages to preach on, isolated excerpts for "Bible study," and individual verses to serve as popular sound bites. The Bible is a big book, so they can pick and choose what they wish to put on display. They do little to facilitate a genuine encounter with the Scripture. Why? Because preachers recognize that if they presented the Bible openly, honestly, and completely, if they encouraged us to read and think for ourselves, people would raise a lot of questions—difficult questions, ones for which they would not have nice, neat answers. This makes pastors uncomfortable; they have little to gain from this scenario and much to lose. They know that people desire definite answers, decisive responses, unhesitating replies which settle issues conclusively. Ambiguity and uncertainty are not popular. Doubts and questions do not fill pews, or pocket books. Thus, preachers continue to dole out a tasty and seasoned Scripture week after week.

And let me be clear. I am not talking about one specific kind of preacher or Christian denomination. They all do it— fundamentalists, evangelicals, Pentecostals, main stream moderates, left wing liberals, emergent church pastors, prosperity preachers, mega-church celebrities, mini-church part-timers, and the list goes on and on. No one serves up the Scripture uncooked. Rather than boldly and bluntly lay it out for us, we get sanitized sermons that bowdlerize the Bible because they don't want to offend or unnerve anyone.

There is, in fact, a long, long history of covering up the complexity of the Bible—like a woman in Saudi Arabia. The Church has always had a vested interest in who reads the Scripture. For years, they allowed Bibles to be printed only in Latin or Greek. Since most people could not read those languages, they were dependent on the priests to tell them what was in the Bible and to interpret it for them. Martin Luther and the Protestant reformers argued that everyone should have access to Scripture. Nearly 500 years later, Luther would presumably be pleased to know that not only is the Bible the all time best seller, but it is also the best seller year after year. The average American household owns three Bibles, the average Christian American household six (and the average North Korean zero). Think about it: That is more Bibles than TVs! Millions and millions of Bibles are purchased each year. Copies of Scripture are ubiquitous.

But of course no one actually reads the Bible. It's like Tocqueville's *Democracy in America* — surely everyone says they've read it, but no one really has. Those who do read the Bible have only examined parts of it. It is estimated that fewer than ten percent of Christians have read the whole thing. Biblical literacy has all but vanished. Many of my students come from Christian backgrounds, but they lack basic knowledge about the Bible. It is truly unfortunate when they approach me and say, "Why didn't they ever tell me that in Sunday school?" or "Does my preacher know about this passage?" or "Wow, I had no idea that was in the Bible."

These students have never read the Scripture for themselves and they have been fed a highly selective, sugarcoated version of it. When they arrive in my class, or many like them at other colleges, universities, and seminaries, they meet the unexpurgated Bible for the first time. They react to it in various ways: shock, amusement, excitement, outrage, confusion — and occasional apathy from the D- student. Most, at some level, are utterly appalled. Indeed, we may not always like what we find in the Bible. But when you love someone, you tell them not what they want to hear, but what they need to hear. When you love God and God's word, it requires that you reveal the truth, even if it hurts. At first, the light might be painfully blinding. But surely knowing what's in Scripture is preferable to remaining in the dark, unenlightened. Yes, ignorance is bliss, and bliss can be, well, blissful. But if we as Christians desire to grow in our faith, we must read the Bible and deal candidly with it. And that may not always be blissful.

A WORD OF ENCOURAGEMENT

Though it may not always be fun and games, pizza and ice cream, the unabridged Bible is better for us. Better because it will nourish and enrich our spiritual, ethical, and communal lives. Partaking of God's unrefined Revelation cultivates one's own personal faith, not the one given to us by parents, preachers, or friends. For faith to be meaningful, we must take ownership of it. The best way to make it our own is to pick up the knife and fork and dig into the Word for ourselves, rejecting the sweetened, pureed, and spooned version. Taking it raw will not only strengthen our faith, but it will also make us better people. Mulling over the complexity of Scripture, struggling to digest its tasteless elements helps us wrestle with the messiness of life itself. It makes us more sensitive to the difficulties and diversity of perspectives in the world around us. It will help us love others.

And it will make us a better body of believers. The unprocessed Bible inevitably prompts thoughts and questions, which leads naturally to conversation. Exchanging ideas, doubts, and concerns with other people about issues raised by the Bible fosters a genuine sense of community.

Sure, there's the occasional church split, but for the most part, when we dialogue with open hearts and a gentle spirit, we will connect with others on a profounder level. Challenges forge substantive relationships. Spirited discussion is invigorating and healthy. If nothing else, we must have some intimate knowledge of the Bible in order to prevent being misled by preachers. We can spot the cooked version much more easily if we know what it tastes like raw. Besides, it is simply best to be honest. Who can argue with sincerity, integrity, and the pursuit of truth?

The Bible itself summons us to undertake such a pursuit, to embrace a richer, more complex faith. In Genesis 32 we read a story in which Jacob wrestles with God. We aren't told if it's judo, MMA, or free-style, but the guy is fighting against the deity. After the contest, God changes his name from Jacob to Israel, which means "one who strives with God." The very name Israel, then, means to struggle and contend with the Almighty. Woven into the fabric of our tradition, into the name itself, is the notion of active engagement with God, not passive compliance. Just like Jacob, we too are free to—called to—stand up and say what we think, express our thoughts, tussle with the Lord. Arguing with God is a form, perhaps the highest form, of faith. By marked contrast, the word Muslim means "one who submits to God." We as Christians belong to the tradition of vigorous struggle, not docile submission. Not that there is anything wrong with submission—or women in Saudi Arabia covering themselves—but it's simply not our heritage.

Furthermore, it's not just Jacob. The Bible features many characters who engage in lively debate with God. Abraham, employing his moral reasoning, points out the injustice of God's plan to destroy every inhabitant of Sodom (Genesis

18). What if there are righteous people in the city as well, Abraham asks. Surely, God should not destroy the good folks along with the bad. God listens to Abraham and agrees with him. God embraces the conversation; he does not scold Abraham for disputing his word. There are, to be sure, many other biblical figures who are contentious and doubtful of God. One thinks — or at least I do — of Moses resisting God's call to lead the people out of Egypt (Exodus 3-6), Job's long speeches of protest toward and lament to God (Job 3, 12-14, 16), Isaiah and Jeremiah expressing reluctance to carry out God's mission (Isaiah 6; Jeremiah 1), Jeremiah becoming utterly disillusioned with God (Jeremiah 20), Jonah blatantly rejecting God's call, and then getting angry when God showed mercy to Nineveh (Jonah 1, 4), Gideon demanding that God give him proof of his presence before going to battle (Judges 6), Samuel failing to recognize God's voice and expressing anger over divine decisions (1 Samuel 3, 15), Elijah's frustration from God's lack of support (1 Kings 19), Habakkuk questioning God's justice (Habakkuk 1), the poet of the book of Lamentations indicting God for abandoning his people (Lamentations 2), and the writers of certain psalms charging God with cruelty (Psalm 44, 88).

If you are not familiar with all of these biblical texts, stop reading, grab your Bible, or your phone, and examine each of these passages. Now.

✦ ✦ ✦ ✦

Did you do it?

See what I mean, the Bible is not full of yes-men who acquiesce to God without any thought or hesitation. Rather, it's replete with characters — including spunky women — who challenge God, who struggle and wrestle with God, who express their own sentiments, even, or especially, when they are at odds with the deity's. The Bible, it seems, is calling us to develop this kind of relationship with God — and the Word of God — a relationship marked with questions, protests, doubts, and fears. It may be a messy relationship, but it's an authentic one.

At the heart of our Christian faith is the belief that God became a human in the person of Jesus Christ. God entered the fray of human existence. He entered into our time and space and experienced the muddled social, cultural, literary, political, and religious arenas of life. Maybe part of the truth of the Incarnation is that we can — must — relate to God with our humanity, at the very center of which is our mind, our ability to reflect and reason, amidst the complexity of human existence. Struggling with the Bible, then, is part of embracing the fundamental truth of the Incarnation.

Jesus himself teaches that we are to love God with all of our heart, soul, *and mind* (Matthew 22:37; Luke 10:27). Our intellect must be part of the fully lived religious life. Using our God-given capacities to contemplate the Word of God is surely something God Incarnate beckons us to do. Paul writes: "When I was a child, I spoke like a child, I thought like a child, I reasoned like a child; but when I became an adult, I put away childish things" (1 Corinthians 13:8). Just as life is easier for children (at least in many ways — learning long division not being one of them), so too it is easier to continue being spoon fed the Bible by preachers who are happy to oblige. But we need to put an end to the childish ways of approaching the Word; it's time to follow Paul and be adults.

It's time to be like the Bereans who are praised for "examining the Scriptures every day to see if what Paul said was true" (Acts 17:11). They are applauded not for accepting what they were taught, but rather for assaying the Scripture to see if it matched up with what they heard from the pulpit. It is true that this can be arduous work. The Bible is a long and sometimes demanding book. Reading takes time and energy; thinking is hard, which is why the diluted version from the preacher is so tempting. But we must resist. We must love God with our minds.

Real adult faith requires real reading. And you can do it. There are 775,630 words in the Bible (I counted them, each one), give or take, depending on the translation. If you read at the average rate of 200-250 words per minute, you can work through the entire Bible in about 60 hours. If you read for a measly ten to twelve minutes a day, or about one hour a week, you could go through it in a year. If you read for two hours a day — instead of playing Angry Birds — you could read it in a month. I stress the importance of reading the Bible because I don't want you to read this book and think that you now know everything that you haven't been told, or that you've been suitably informed. Don't rely on preachers, teachers, or scholars. And certainly don't trust me. Listen to what others have to offer, but don't take them at their word. Be suspicious; be bold enough to think. Read. Question. Explore. Doubt. Probe. It's okay. It's part of loving God.

In order to do this, we must approach Scripture with an open mind. We cannot decide what we think before we taste the raw Revelation. We cannot put the cart before the horse, the rickshaw before the runner. A sincere encounter with the Word of God requires that we not start with a certain set of presuppositions or beliefs and then force the Bible to fit those assumptions. Too many Christians begin with the conclusion and then twist themselves and Scripture into knots trying to defend their conclusion. Surely God does not want us to do that. If you look at each instance where horses appear in the Bible, not once is the cart before it. There are no rickshaws in Scripture.

Being open can be difficult. New things can be frightening, intimidating. When we read God's Word unedited, our spiritual palates will discover new flavors and textures, many of which we may not like. We may have thoughts and queries that have never crossed our minds before. Some aspects of our faith may become more tentative; certainty may suddenly be more elusive. We may find ourselves in a world of gray instead of black and white. Changing to a raw diet may be an unsettling, even scary experience — and humans are not naturally drawn to such experiences. It is human nature to prefer familiarity, safety, and security, and so that is what religious leaders give us. They tell us that the Bible contains the answers to life's most complicated questions, that it's a wonderful guidebook for living, that it declares that God wants us to have our best possible life (now), that it proclaims Jesus' love for each of us. But it isn't and it doesn't. Really, it doesn't say that God loves everyone or that Jesus loves you. That's the cooked version to which we have grown accustomed. That's what fills churches week after week: the promise of a delicious snack that is easy to digest.

But we must demand the real thing. We must learn to take it raw. Yes, the cooked version goes down smoothly, but it's also depleted of many valuable minerals and nutrients necessary for a vibrant life of faith. The raw Bible will nourish a stronger, more robust, responsible faith, even if assimilating it is a less pleasant experience. Yes, the unedited, undiluted version will be taxing and risky, but it also brings the potential for real spiritual vitality. Yes, the raw food may very well make us sick at first; it is, after all, an acquired taste (no, not like beer). Some in fact may never acquire it; some may be so disgusted by the unprocessed version that they cannot go on. There is more than one story of the Christian who studies the Scripture in depth for the first time and ends up rejecting it. That may happen to a few. But if you don't take that risk, it's not your faith — it's a faith that has been given to you. And that's not a faith worth having.

Our Judeo-Christian heritage has had many voices who called people to move beyond a secure, easy life of conventionality. Beginning with the Old Testament prophets who were critical of Israel's institutions, its leaders, and religious beliefs and practices, our tradition is filled with those who cared enough to criticize the status quo, to cry for change, and issue challenges. Jesus himself confronted the religious authorities of his day and summoned people to a more genuine, and riskier, religious life. The call for the clergy — and all of us Christians — to stop serving and consuming a bogus Bible stands in this long line of counter voices. There's nothing new in this book — just another invitation to live an authentic life before God.

The present book is fairly straightforward. It serves the Bible raw in a six course meal. Not the conventional number of courses, I know, but then the Bible is not a conventional book. We will simply examine what the Bible says, and what it does not say. There's little or no technical commentary or elaborate analysis. You don't need a PhD to dine with us — you don't even need a GED. It's not a book that reveals secret meanings to the original Hebrew or Greek words, exposes heretofore unknown interpretations, or uncovers hidden facts about the Bible. Everything is right there on the table; we must only be willing to partake. But that is up to you. I cannot do that for you. I am here to show you the wonderfully raw spread. I am merely the waiter, so to speak. (Hi, I am Mark, I'll be taking care of you this evening.) I can lay the uncooked Bible before you, but you have to join in. You must read and reflect for yourself. You must find your own answers — and more importantly, your own questions. Or as Paul says, you must work out your own salvation. My objective is to place the Bible in the center of the table and start the conversation around it — but it's just a start.

Indeed, one of my main goals is to encourage you to do more studying and research. I hope to drive you to libraries, to your local college, to your pastor or priest, to your friends and colleagues to hear their ideas and opinions. Heck, just start with Google. The point is that you must do more work; you must actively participate in the conversation. Hopefully, your encounter with the uncensored Bible marks the beginning of a sustained relationship with Scripture, not the end. My desire is that that relationship begins to set you free — free to love God with your mind like so many biblical characters, including Jesus himself, free to have an adult faith with all of its potential perils and joys, and free to love each other with all of our doubts and difficulties.

One final point is worth stressing before we begin. This book is not about my trying to convince you what to think about the Bible. It's about my trying to convince you what to think about: the Bible. The colon in that last sentence is as indispensable as the one in your body — we'd be starting with a big mess if we took it out. This book is about the Bible, not about my attempt to persuade you to interpret it my way. Frankly, I am not even sure what "my way" is ninety percent of the time — and the other half I really have no clue. I will add my "raw reflections" at the end of each chapter, some of my own personal ways of wrestling with the text, but my thoughts and suggestions are always tentative, at best, and my voice is only one among many. So again, it's not about me. But in case you are interested, here is a brief word about who I am.

My story is fairly typical. I grew up in a Christian home and went to a conservative Christian school for thirteen years where my father was a teacher and coach. I was diligently taught the Bible from a very young age. While I was not a true "Bible thumper" or "preacher boy," I certainly said and did all the right things. I toed the party line. I went to church, did my "devotions," said my memory verses, witnessed to others, didn't curse or drink or have sex with my girlfriends — okay, girlfriend. In retrospect, though, I am not sure how much of it was my own. Church, prayer, and Bible study were just something we did. I never thought much about it. I was too busy with sports. Then I went to college to play baseball and major in something useful like communications, or maybe biology.

In the first semester, I enrolled in the required introductory Bible class and undertook for the first time a critical and academic study of Scripture. I knew the Bible well, but I had never approached it this way before. I realize now that I was getting my first taste of it untreated. I was intrigued, fascinated, and disturbed. Suddenly, things weren't so simple. I began to read and think for myself. I began to analyze and scrutinize. I began to cultivate my own faith. And I continue to do all these things today. I have not figured it all out. I still have many more questions than satisfactory answers. My life of faith is a constant struggle with God and his Word. It's a process, a journey that commenced when I first encountered raw Revelation. It was, and is, life changing.

COURSE 1

THE BIBLE

The first course of our meal introduces us to one fundamental feature of the Bible: its diversity. This initial serving whets our appetite and primes us for what follows. To ease us in, we'll start by focusing on some familiar texts, namely, the stories of creation, Christmas, and Easter. Though the stories may be well-known, they will taste differently when we encounter them fresh. Specifically, we will get a sense of the complexity, and indeed, inconsistency, of Scripture.

We are programmed, it seems, to want consistency in our lives. We want it from parents, teachers, politicians, pastors, judges, and other sources of authority and leadership. We value reliability, stability, and dependability — even though we know how hard it is to achieve. If you are a parent, for instance, you understand the difficulties of being regular—not to mention how challenging it is to be consistent with your children. A reliable politician? A consistent referee? A stable schizophrenic? Just not going to happen very often. Perhaps, then, that is why we would really like for those to be characteristics of the Bible. But they are not. We desire a pillar of certainty amidst our shifting world. Instead, the Scripture is uneven and bumpy, varied and paradoxical. So we must deal with it. But churches don't. Instead, they boil down the variety of Scripture into one smooth, homogenous soup. Much is lost as a result.

I am purposefully eschewing the word "contradiction" in our discussion—and I should also probably eschew the word "eschew" while I am at it. I am not using the term "contradiction" because of all the negative connotations surrounding it. When people say that the Bible is "contradictory" or that it has "contradictions," they are usually trying to denigrate the Scripture. But to say that the Bible is contradictory is pointless and misguided because it implies or assumes that it should be "pro-dictory," or whatever the opposite term is. But that is a foolish expectation. Would you say, for example, that the Supreme Court is contradictory? Of course not, because we know it's composed of different people with different ideas. It's a collection of disparate opinions. The same idea applies to the Bible. It's a diverse compendium of perspectives. It's more like "tri-verse" or "multi-verse"—it's got different "verses" which say different things. But of course it does. And here's why:

The Old Testament is a collection of books written by many different people over a long period of time—at the very least 300 years, and perhaps nearly 1,000 years (that's like, a millennium). It's to be expected that it's not all going to say the same thing all the time. Think of the impossibility of finding complete harmony and consensus on all matters in a collection of literature that spans that length of time. The authors lived in different places, had various beliefs, and particular messages to communicate; they confronted unique situations and problems in disparate social, religious, political, and economic contexts. So of course the Old Testament is going to be "different," that is, inconsistent. But it's not "contradictory."

The same basic facts apply to the New Testament. The time span is a bit shorter; it was written over a roughly one hundred year period (that's like, a century). But it's still a collection of books. Thus, saying that the Bible is contradictory is like saying that the public library is contradictory. It's sort of self-evident. Nonetheless, the Bible's diversity offers an unexpected taste for those anticipating total coherence.

So why, then, do preachers melt down the Bible's incongruities? Two main reasons, I think. First, they raise sticky questions about "what really happened." Our faith is based on specific historical events — the life and death of Jesus, or perhaps a literal seven-day creation for some. If there are conflicting accounts in the Bible, then is one wrong and the other right? How do we know which is which? If part of it is inaccurate, then what, if any, can we trust as reliable history?

Secondly, the Bible also features conflicting viewpoints about a given question or subject, such as how one is "saved" or acquires eternal life, as we will have a chance to sample in later courses. Preachers leave these facts off the platter because they complicate matters. The security of easy answers vanishes when we have more than one choice. Multiplicity erases simplicity. Having two or three options means we have to think, evaluate, and assess. That can be difficult. Most people prefer things to be straightforward and clear-cut, so that is what we get.

Now let's gets real and get it raw.

WHEN DID GOD CREATE EVE?

Everyone knows the first few chapters of the Bible — "In the beginning," the seventh day of rest, Adam, Eve, the snake. It's all very familiar. But perhaps not so familiar is the idea that there are two separate stories of creation. They've been right there the whole time, but no one's ever pointed it out to you. You may wonder how you could have missed them; for it is not difficult to see that two distinct, incompatible accounts of creation have been placed side-by-side.

The first one is the seven-day account; it begins in Genesis 1:1 and ends with the first line of 2:4 ("These are the generations of the heavens and earth when they were created"). The second one is the Garden of Eden story; it begins with the second line of 2:4 ("In the day that the Lord God made the earth and the heavens") and continues to the end of chapter three. I know, it's annoying that the split occurs in the middle of a verse — it gives a new meaning to "diverse" and it also makes me wonder if the guys who put in verse numbers, only about 800 years ago, were trying to hide the two stories. At any rate, it would be good to take a minute to reread Genesis 1-3 for yourself, making note of the sequence in which things are created in the first story in contrast to that in the second.

According to Genesis 1, God (Elohim) creates in the following order:

Day 1: Light

Day 2: Sky

Day 3: Land, plants, trees, vegetation

Day 4: Sun and moon

Day 5: Birds and fish

Day 6: Land animals, man and woman

In the second account, the Lord (Yahweh) God—note the change in divine name—creates in this order:

1) Man created from dust

2) Garden of Eden

3) Trees (including Tree of Knowledge of Good and Evil and Tree of Life)

4) Animals

5) Woman from the rib of man

6) The story of the serpent, the fruit, and the expulsion from the Garden

These are two separate narratives. If we try to harmonize them, it simply does not work. Either humans were created at the very end of the story, at the same time, after the plants and animals, as in Genesis 1. Or the man was created first by himself before the plants and animals, and then after none of the animals were found to be a suitable companion for the man—for which I personally am very grateful—the Lord formed the woman, as in Genesis 2. It could not have literally happened both ways.

Two other differences are nearly impossible to reconcile. First, when God created the man and woman in Genesis 1, he declared to them that *"every* seed bearing plant on the face of the *whole* earth and *every* fruit bearing tree"* was theirs for food (1:29). But in the second story, the Lord forbids the man to eat from the Tree of Knowledge of Good and Evil. Is one tree off limits or not? Secondly, the very beginning of the second story makes it clear that "no shrub of the field had yet appeared on the earth and no plant of the field had yet sprung up" before the man was created (2:5-7). This does not fit with the first account in which "the land produced vegetation, plants bearing seed according to their kind" (1:12) on the third day, well prior to the creation of humans on the sixth day.

Some may argue that the first story is a broad overview and that the second is a detailed focus on the creation of humans. In fact, some translations, such as the popular New International Version (NIV), try to suggest this by rendering the verbs in the second story in the plu-perfect tense instead of the simple past (I promise I won't ever say "plu-perfect" again after this paragraph). For example, if we translate Genesis 2:19 with the plu-perfect, "Now the Lord God *had formed* out of the ground all the beasts of the field and all the birds of the air," it appears as though the text is referring back to days five and six in the first story. It implies that the animals were already created and the Lord is now bringing them to the man to be named. But if we translate, as most Bibles do, the simple past tense ("formed" instead of "had formed"), then the Lord is creating the animals for the first time, after the man has already been made, which makes the scenario quite different from Genesis 1. But regardless of which tense you choose—or even if you are relaxed—the two stories cannot be merged, at least not without torturing the text and our basic sense of logic and reasoning.

So how might we ruminate on this unfiltered idea? Let me make a few suggestions here and now, as opposed to holding them to the end of the chapter as I will do for the subsequent courses. After all, this is your first taste, and I want to be an encouraging, supportive waiter who keeps you at the table. Plus, I think I actually have a few helpful ideas in this instance, which will not always be the case when we deal with the upcoming heavier, really raw material.

If Genesis 1-3 is logically, rationally, literally, and — we could add in light of contemporary debates — scientifically incoherent, does that make these stories false, untrue? Are they nothing more than make-believe? Perhaps. But maybe Genesis 1-3 is not about scientific, logical, and rational truth. Maybe it is about religious, spiritual, and theological truth. Surely whoever is responsible for the final form of Genesis 1-3 was fully aware of the differences between the two accounts. The tensions and discrepancies apparently did not matter to them, from which we can deduce that they were not attempting to provide a logically and scientifically accurate account of how the world literally began. Instead, they were trying to express truths about God, God's relationship to the world, the value of humans, and the like. Simply because the stories are rationally inconsistent does not make them untrue.

If we read Genesis 1-3 looking for literal, scientific truths, we are, I would propose, fundamentally misunderstanding the kind of truth the text is conveying. It would be tantamount to reading a few consecutive pages from a dictionary (not dictionary.com) and concluding that it is a terrible novel with no plot or character development. Or like looking at a page from a phone book (as if anyone still uses those) and declaring that it is out of balance because the number in the bottom right hand corner is not the sum total of all the other numbers in the column. In each case, we would be misreading the type of information, the genre of truth, that the document intends to convey. It would be incorrect to judge a dictionary by the standards of a novel, or a phone book by those of a balance sheet. In the same way, we should not evaluate Genesis 1-3 in terms of literal, scientific, rational truth. By juxtaposing two incongruous stories, the text itself is telling us loudly and clearly that it cannot be judged on those terms. So if you were to ask me if I believed Genesis 1-3 to be true, I would say, "Absolutely." But I don't believe them to be scientifically true.

Perhaps, then, you might ask for an example of a theological, religious, or spiritual truth conveyed by Genesis 1-3 — or maybe you wouldn't. But if you did, it would be a very difficult question to answer in limited space. But I might say something like this: Humans, all humans, are made in the image of God (even Osama bin Laden and Roseanne Barr). Genesis 1 teaches that each and every person has equal value and worth because we are all made in the likeness of the deity. This is a practical, moral, and spiritual truth with ramifications for how we live our day-to-day lives. It has tremendous implications for how we treat other people. Thus, Genesis 1 is deeply relevant and meaningful for us today. But it's not relevant in biology class.

We've got time for one truth from the second story as well: In an ideal world, we would be nudists — since Adam and Eve only get clothes after they sinned. This truth may not be as profound as the previous one, and I'd have to disagree with it in light of our obesity epidemic. Actually, though, the story is probably giving us a fairly meaningful answer to the question, "Why do we humans, unlike all the animals, wear clothes?" The answer seems to be that we are creatures with a moral dimension; thus we must cover up because we can make unethical decisions.

Once you stop thinking about naked people, you might well start to think that if we are to interpret the creation stories in terms of moral and theological truth rather than scientific, logical truth, then what in Scripture can be taken literally? What can we trust as a reliable historical record? Where does one draw the line between what's literal and what's not? Is the whole Bible to be read on the theological and spiritual level? It's one thing to read Genesis 1-3 symbolically because it is, after all, a story about events at which no one was present — Adam and Eve did not write Genesis 1-3. But it's an altogether different situation to point to the discrepancies in the Gospels — purportedly the historical records of the life of Jesus — and declare that such inconsistencies compel us to read them too as conveying religious truths, not historical ones. If there are inconsistencies in the Gospels, can we trust them as reliable? If they are not accurate history, then on what is our faith based?

Good questions. Hard questions. Raw questions which don't have effortless answers.

WHAT DID THE WISE MEN SAY TO THE SHEPHERDS?

It is quite striking that the Old Testament begins with two creation stories and the New Testament begins with four gospels. It is almost as though the Bible itself is screaming for us to recognize its diversity and resulting inconsistencies. As has long been noted, there are a variety of irreconcilable elements among the four gospels, including a number in the crucial stories of Jesus' birth and his death and resurrection.

Just as Genesis 1-3 is a well-known text, so too the birth stories of Jesus are familiar, yet hardly anyone realizes that the Christmas stories in Matthew and Luke are entirely distinct and virtually impossible to harmonize. Again, it does not require an advanced degree to see this; it simply takes a few minutes of comparing Matthew 1-2 with Luke 1-2. Why don't you take a moment to do that now; read those chapters with a brand new pair of lenses and see what you find.

According to Matthew, the story goes this way:

Mary and Joseph are engaged when Mary becomes pregnant.

An angel tells Joseph that the child is from the Holy Spirit.

Jesus is born in Bethlehem.

The wise men follow a star to Bethlehem.

The wise men meet Herod.

The wise men go to see Jesus.

Joseph is warned in a dream of Herod's intent to kill Jesus.

Joseph, Mary, and Jesus flee to Egypt.

They return when Herod dies.

Here is an outline of Luke's story:

Mary conceives by the Holy Spirit.

Mary and Joseph journey from Nazareth to Bethlehem for the census.

Mary gives birth to Jesus in a manger.

The angel announces the birth to shepherds who go to see Jesus.

The Bible

Mary and Joseph take Jesus to the temple in Jerusalem. They return home to Nazareth.

These are two separate stories. Luke mentions no wise men, magical star (how does a star stop over a single house?), Herod, or the flight to Egypt. Matthew makes no reference to the census (who takes a census that creates the bureaucratic nightmare of everyone returning to their hometown just to be counted?), the manger, angels in the sky and the shepherds, or the trip to the temple. Indeed, it is very difficult to imagine that Matthew and Luke knew about the events reported in each other's story and simply chose not to mention them in their own account. Especially Luke who begins his gospel by declaring that he has "carefully investigated" all matters (Luke 1:1-4).

The church's version of the Christmas story is a combination of the two accounts, as is the typical nativity scene which places shepherds (Luke) and wise men (Matthew) at the manger (Luke). We typically encounter these narratives during the Christmas season, so, easy as it might be to compare them, we'd rather, quite understandably, have another cup of eggnog, sing one more carol, and get a kiss under the mistletoe — though not necessarily in that order. It is true that a close textual analysis of Matthew and Luke does not make for great Christmas party conversation. Thus, the issue that is routinely overlooked is that logically, historically the two disparate versions cannot be merged. In both stories Jesus is born in Bethlehem (though Matthew says nothing about the manger), but where does he go after that — to Egypt to escape from Herod's murderous threats or to the temple in Jerusalem to be circumcised? It can't be both. Luke 2:39 states clearly that after their trip to the temple, Jesus and

27

his family return home to Nazareth; they don't go to Egypt. Jesus, in short, cannot be two places at once — okay maybe Jesus could, but Mary and Joseph couldn't.

So what if we tried to combine the two accounts. Is there any way to harmonize them so that both are literally accurate? Only if one resorts to a highly strained scenario which makes little sense and sounds nothing like the Christmas story we all know. Basically, one would have to place Matthew's story after Luke's like this: Mary and Joseph left their home in Nazareth and traveled to Bethlehem where Jesus was born in a manger. Then the family went to Jerusalem to present Jesus in the temple a few days later, after which they returned home to Nazareth. At some point in the next two years, unmentioned by any gospel writer and for no reason whatsoever, Jesus and his family made the long and unnecessary trip — especially with a two-year old confined to his donkey-seat — back to Bethlehem, since they must be there to meet the wise men who have have been faithfully following the star this entire time; then Jesus and his family journeyed to Egypt to escape from Herod, before returning and settling in Nazareth. This would be one bizarre itinerary: from Nazareth, to Bethlehem, to Jerusalem, back home to Nazareth, back to Bethlehem again, to Egypt, and back to Nazareth again. Mary and Joseph need a new travel agent.

But, alas, even if we go through these tortuous harmonizing gymnastics, we still can't get there — wherever there is supposed to be. Matthew 2:22-23 won't let us. In this passage, Mary and Joseph and Jesus are coming back from Egypt and they would like to return to their home in Judea (where Bethlehem is located). But Herod's son is ruling over that region, and Joseph is warned in a dream that he should go instead to the district of Galilee, which he does, settling "in a town called Nazareth." Here it is evident that for Matthew Jesus was not living in Nazareth prior to his flight to Egypt, otherwise he would have said, "Joseph and his family returned to their home in Nazareth." Instead, Matthew assumes that Mary and Joseph lived in Judea prior to their flight and that they moved for the first time to Nazareth upon their return—which makes our hypothetical synthesized version untenable. Thus, even if we resort to the weirdest of Christmas stories, we cannot reconcile Matthew and Luke's accounts of Jesus' birth.

So how are we to digest this? One way is to suggest that Matthew and Luke's main objective was not to write accurate history, but rather to express truth about the significance of Jesus. Matthew and Luke, the proposal goes, were writing religious history or theological history, not history as we think of it in terms of accurate reporting of events of the past. Thus, both accounts could be true theologically and religiously even though they are incongruous historically. Yes, if you are paying attention, this is essentially the same "solution" we proposed with the creation stories.

What then is an example of a religious or theological truth, if not historical, in the Christmas stories? Several aspects of Matthew's narrative recall the Old Testament story of Moses in Exodus 1-2. Most notably, Herod's attempt to kill the babies in Bethlehem is reminiscent of Pharaoh's injunction to destroy the Israelite infants. The theological (not historical) truth that Matthew expresses with his story is that Jesus is a new type of Moses—a lawgiver, prophet, priest, and savior. Like Moses, Jesus came to earth to instruct, intercede for, and save the people. That is Matthew's point; he's not trying to tell you what actually happened when Jesus was born. He's conveying a message about the meaning, purpose, and identity of Jesus. After all, would a sensible governor like Herod—or even a totally stupid one — whose job it was to keep order and peace really command the massacre of countless innocent babies (and it not be mentioned by any other writer in antiquity, including the Bible)? No. But that is how Matthew tells the story, not because it really happened, but because Matthew is announcing to his audience the arrival of a new Moses.

But the risk in making this type of argument about the birth narratives is much greater than making it with the creation stories. If Matthew and Luke are not historically accurate — as their inconsistencies show — then what, if anything, in the Gospels can we hang our hat on as being a reliable account of what really happened? Do we have to give up wearing hats? Do we have to abandon history altogether? Do we choose between Matthew and Luke's account? Could there be some literal history and some theology mixed together? If so, how do we decide? These are tough questions with no easy answers. Be we cannot continue to enjoy the synthesized version and pretend the discrepancies don't exist.

WHAT HAPPENED TO EASTER?

When we come to the end of Jesus' life, we have a true murder mystery, for there are four unique accounts, not just two. It is nearly impossible to use the four gospels — and occasionally Acts — to piece together a coherent time line of events from Jesus' triumphal entry into Jerusalem, to his arrest, trial, sentencing, crucifixion, and resurrection. If you don't have time right now to read through the final chapters of all four gospels, you might examine one, which will help prepare you for the following quick run-through of some of the disagreements. Hang on:

In Matthew 21:2-6, Mark 11:2-7, and Luke 19:30-35 the disciples find and bring a donkey to Jesus for him to ride on as he makes his entrance into Jerusalem. In John 12:14, Jesus himself finds the ass.

The fate of Judas Iscariot is ambiguous, though it certainly is not good. According to Matthew 27:3-10, when Judas realized he had betrayed Jesus, he repented, returned to the temple and threw down the thirty pieces of silver, and then departed and hanged himself. The chief priests take the money and buy a field. Quite differently, in Acts 1:16-19, Judas himself bought the field with the money before his bowels burst open and he died. (This makes for a good Bible version of the game "Would you rather?")

Even the fundamental fact regarding the day of the crucifixion is disputed. According to Mark, Jesus was crucified the day after the Passover meal was eaten (Mark 14:12 and 15:25), whereas John claims that it was before the Passover meal (John 19:14). Hence the oft-spoken line by professors in introductory New Testament classes: In Mark (and Matthew and Luke) Jesus *eats* the Passover meal; in John he *is* the Passover meal, that is, the slain Lamb of God.

Who carried the cross? In Matthew 27:32, Mark 15:21, and Luke 23:36 Simon of Cyrene carried Jesus' cross for him; but according to John 19:17 Jesus bore it by himself.

There are differing reports regarding the two criminals who were crucified with Jesus. According to Matthew 27:44, both men taunted him. But in Luke 23:39-42, only one mocked him while the other one defended him.

There is conflicting information about what Jesus was offered to drink just before his death: vinegar (Matthew 27:48; Luke 23:36; John 19:29) or wine mixed with myrrh (Mark 15:23). In Mark, Jesus does not drink what is offered; in John he does.

Jesus' last words are reported differently. In Matthew 27:46 and Mark 15:34 they are "My God, my God, why have you forsaken me?" In Luke 23:46 they are "Father, into your hands I commend my spirit," and in John 19:30, he says, "It is finished."

The tearing of the temple curtain occurs at different times. In Luke 23:45 it rips before Jesus dies, but in Matthew 27:51 and Mark 15:38 it happens after his death.

After Jesus has died, the Roman centurion makes different statements. In Matthew 27:54 and Mark 15:39 he claims that Jesus was the Son of God, a theological assertion. In Luke 23:47, he observes, "Truly this man was innocent," a legal or judicial pronouncement.

Discrepancies occur in the sign that was placed over Jesus' head. According to Matthew 27:37, it read, "This is Jesus, the King of the Jews." According to Mark 15:26, it states only, "The King of the Jews." Luke 23:38 says, "This is the King of the Jews," and in John 19:19, "Jesus of Nazareth, the King of the Jews." Minor differences, perhaps, but it was only a few words, and, here's the kicker, the words were written down: It shouldn't have been difficult for all four writers to get it correct. It wasn't dialogue that might have been misheard or a brief occurrence that might not have been seen. The sign was there the whole time, and the gospels still don't agree. This discrepancy, by the way, illustrates the problem with arguing that the differences that we've mentioned so far can be explained by positing that they all occurred and that each writer only told part of the story. Do we honestly think there were four different signs above Jesus' head?

Now on to Easter. There are two basic consistencies here. One, the tomb was empty; and two, there were no bunnies or multi-colored eggs involved.

According to all four gospels, women were the first to arrive at Jesus' tomb, though specifically how many and which ones is unclear from Matthew 28:1, Mark 16:1, and Luke 23:55-24:10. John's version is the most unique because it's only Mary Magdalene (20:1). In Matthew, the stone was still in place when the women get to the grave. Then an angel descends and rolls it away (28:1-2). By contrast, in the other three accounts, the women find the stone already removed (Mark 16:4; Luke 24:2; John 20:1).

The number, appearance, and location of divine beings are different. There is one angel in Matthew who sits on the stone; Mark 16:5 records that the women saw "a young man, dressed in a white robe" sitting inside the tomb on the right side. Luke 24:4 says that "two men in dazzling white clothes stood beside them." In John 20:12, Mary encountered "two angels in white, sitting where the body of Jesus had been lying, one at the head and the other at the feet."

The words that the divine being(s) say to the women varies somewhat in Matthew, Mark, and Luke. But they essentially announce that Jesus is raised and instruct them to go tell his disciples. The women's response, however, diverges, as well as what happens next. In Matthew, the women run to tell the others, but on their way, Jesus himself meets them, and he too enjoins them to go tell his followers (28:8-9). In Luke, the women do not meet Jesus on their way to tell the others. When the disciples hear the news from the women, they do not believe them and only Peter goes to check out the tomb (24:9-12). In Mark, in stark contrast, the women "said nothing to anyone" (16:8). In John, before Mary encounters the angel, she runs to tell Peter and "the other disciple" that the body has been stolen. Both men run back to the tomb, see for themselves, don't understand what has happened, and return home (20:2-10). Then Jesus appears to Mary alone.

There are other discrepancies we could point to among the various accounts, such as Jesus' dialogue during his trials with the Jewish leaders and with Pilate, but this list can suffice. How could all these conflicting pieces of information about Jesus' crucifixion and resurrection be historically accurate? We aren't talking about a couple of obscure inconsistencies in some minor gospel passages. We are talking about numerous tensions in the four accounts of the most significant event in Christianity. It is, in short, impossible — at least if one remains within the realm of reason — to reconcile the varying accounts of Jesus' crucifixion and resurrection.

There are also a couple of other incredible events that are mentioned by only one of the gospel writers, so they do not qualify as discrepancies, but they do raise the question: If it really happened, how or why would only one writer report it? For example, only Matthew writes that at the moment of Jesus' death there was an earthquake in which tombs were opened and many dead bodies came to life. After Jesus' resurrection these also-resurrected people came out of their graves, entered Jerusalem, and appeared to many (Matthew 27:53). This is surely the most amazing event surrounding the crucifixion, but only Matthew bothers to note it! How is it possible that not one other writer of the entire New Testament references it in any fashion? Moreover, imagine the massive and immediate impact such an occurrence would have made if it had actually occurred? Is Matthew really telling us what really happened?

My guess, by the way, is that you were largely unaware of this zombie part of the story, even though you have faithfully been to church every Easter Sunday and seen some Easter dramas. Preachers and play-writes don't include it, though I am not sure why. Maybe it's because they don't want to combine Halloween and Easter. Maybe it's because it is too far-fetched and unhistorical for our tastes. It's as if Matthew has embarrassingly gone too far in his story-telling. And plus, it might scare the little children.

WHO KILLED GOLIATH?

Before moving on to the next course, let's go back to the Old Testament for a minute and sample a few more items just for the fun of it. There are countless conflicts between names and numbers when we compare various biblical genealogies and numerical data. But let's skip over all of them, save two.

Who killed Goliath? According to 1 Samuel 17, it was David of course. But 2 Samuel 21:19 says it was Elhanan. One might posit that there were two guys named Goliath— David killed one and Elhanan the other. It seems clear, however, that these two texts refer to the same Goliath, as both declare that his spear was as large as a weaver's beam— a statement Freud would certainly enjoy. Or maybe one could circumvent the problem by asserting that Elhanan is another name for David. But wouldn't it be odd to call David David throughout 2 Samuel, and then all of a sudden call him Elhanan in one verse. At any rate, Elhanan got the shaft when it comes to fame and fortune as no one remembers him as the slayer of the giant.

How many of each animal did Noah take onto the ark? Everyone knows that the animals went in two-by-two, as it says in Genesis 6:20. But according to Genesis 7:2-3, Noah took seven pairs of the clean animals and one pair of the unclean—that's a lot more work for Noah on the boat, not to mention a lot less room for the animals. I suspect the two-by-two tradition stuck because (a) who wants to try to explain "clean" and "unclean" when telling the story to children, and (b) it means each animal had one and only one mate—it's like the animals are monogamous— whereas if you have, say, seven boy lions and seven girl lions, there's going to be some hanky-panky. Thus, the seven-by-seven tradition has been washed away.

The books of 1-2 Samuel and 1-2 Kings record the history of Israel. The books of 1-2 Chronicles are a second history, written later, by different people, probably in a different place, with a different agenda. So there are two separate, independent histories of Israel in the Old Testament—reminiscent of multiple histories of the life of Jesus (the four gospels). It's déjà vu all over again.

There are in fact a number of places where we can watch the Chronicler reading the books of Samuel and Kings, copying it word for word, but then changing, deleting, or adding elements. One such example is 1 Chronicles 21 which changes 2 Samuel 24. In this story, David takes a census of the people of Israel, and the Lord becomes angry and sends a plague which kills 70,000 Israelites. That's odd. But what makes it particularly odd in Samuel's version is how it starts: "Again the anger of the Lord was kindled against Israel, and he incited David against them, saying: Go count the people of Israel and Judah." Here God provokes David to take the census, David complies, and then God punishes the people severely. Why would God do that?

The writer of 1 Chronicles 21 is clearly struggling with precisely that question. So he rewrites the beginning of the story: "Satan stood up against Israel and incited David to count the people." Ah, now that makes much more sense: Satan tempted David to take the census, David did, and then God became angry. The Chronicler's rewritten version changes one word to make the story more theologically palatable and sensible. It also makes it irreconcilable with the one in Kings.

RAW REFLECTIONS

The Bible is a big, complex book that should not be boiled down to one homogenous mixture. But that is exactly what preachers do when they do not deal with the obvious incongruities found in Scripture. If they do address them, it is typically to harmonize them with sleight-of-hand interpretations. There are no doubt many ways to deep fry the plain meaning of the words with fancy culinary artistry. You know as well as I that people can go to great lengths to make the text say whatever they want, to spin it anyway that suits their needs (think Bill Clinton: "It depends on what 'is' is"). But let's not do that. Let's be honest (think Abe Lincoln). Let's confront our Bible in its raw condition. Imagine, for example, if these incompatible assertions were in another religious text, say, the Koran. What would preachers say? Would they try to synthesize them? Or would they point to them as "mistakes" which prove the inferiority of that sacred text? We must be forthright with ourselves and with our Scripture.

My suggestion for how we might learn to enjoy the Bible's raw inconsistencies—feel free to develop your own—is simply to embrace the complexity. There is no reason to force the wonderful diversity of the Scripture into a single synthetic soup. When we blend and broil the multiple facets of the Bible into one easy-to-swallow concoction, each component loses its unique taste which can be valued independently of the other items on the platter. It's tantamount to smothering each delightfully different delicatessen with chocolate sauce—like a chubby little kid with glasses would do—instead of savoring each morsel on its own.

Now that we've started making fun of children with glandular problems, it's time to switch metaphors (or analogies) for a moment to develop this idea: The Bible is a discussion. It is a conversation of voices which makes it richer, more robust. The Scripture is better, more meaningful, more inspiring, more true-to-life precisely because of its diversity. Would we really want a Bible that is consistent—wouldn't it feel artificial and contrived? Could we really connect with something that does not resonate with the chaos of our lives? Rather, the plurality of voices in Scripture provides it with a sense of dynamism and energy. The Word of God is alive, not static. It is moving, shifting, changing. It is real. It's the Word, but it's made up of words because life is plural.

We need to treat each text of Scripture as we would each person sitting around a table talking—even the chunky kid. Namely, we must listen carefully as we let each one speak for itself. If one person offers an opinion that is at odds with our own or someone else's, we should not be dismissive or respond with, "No, what you really mean is . . ." That is not being kind and sensitive — that is not the right thing to do. In the same way, Christians are misguided when they take the chorus of voices that make up the Bible and compel each one to agree with the others. Or, to switch metaphors yet again, when we take the many beautiful colors of the Bible and mix them into one bland shade.

Reading Scripture, then, is analogous to listening to a debate or sitting around the conference table at a committee meeting. It is a dialogue, not a monologue, and as such, it calls each of us to join the conversation, to listen and interact with the various opinions. The very shape and nature of the Bible summons us to a life of interaction with the Bible, with God, and with each other. The Bible is not a sermon — one voice, one perspective all the time — where we have no opportunity to engage, to participate. Honestly, who wants another sermon? Instead the Bible is an iText, where "i" stands for interface or internet (as in a network of separate but connected pages) or "I" am involved. Listening to a debate or serving on a committee requires more cognition, more mental activity on our part. It's quite the task to consider multiple points of view. We have to think, analyze, critique, and generate insights. That's hard work. But that's what loving God with our mind entails.

A collection of contrasting ideas is precisely what is required to arrive at truth. That is why we form committees and have debates — we know that we need more than one voice to think through the big questions and issues. As world famous physicist Niels Bohr once said: "The opposite of a fact is a falsehood, but the opposite of one profound truth may very well be another profound truth." If truth—profound truth—is paradoxical, the Bible captures it perfectly.

Course 2

GOD

If the Bible is diverse and inconsistent, so is the God who we meet in Scripture. The problem is that preachers cook the Book by sifting out the foul-tasting images of our God. The God presented in church is all-powerful, all-knowing, all-loving, good, holy, and perfect. He is the God we sing about in choruses such as "God is so Good" or "Holy, Holy, Holy" or in the myriad of contemporary praise and worship songs which extol God's attributes of love, mercy, and forgiveness—over and over and over again, in trance-like repetitive refrains. We are assured, without doubt, that God cares about us and wants what is best for us.

Yet when we read the Bible, we encounter a multi-faceted, complex deity who speaks and acts in troubling and disturbing ways. The God we meet in the Word is not all good, holy, loving, and perfect. Christians don't know this because pastors have nothing to gain from our knowing it. It's much nicer and easier for them if we worship a purely wonderful God without the mean, ugly, vindictive characteristics mixed in. Although he is portrayed as both—kind and loving, nasty and brutish—we tend to prefer only the pleasant images, so we are fed a diluted and domesticated deity. The raw images of God never show up on our plates.

As Christians, don't we owe it to God to know what the Scripture reveals about him? How can we worship a God whose nature and character we do not know? How can we claim to want a relationship with God when we haven't even taken the time to read about him, to get to know him? It's true that God may be revealed to us in places outside the Book—perhaps in nature or in quiet meditation, for example. But certainly our Scripture, in its entirety, should be given careful consideration when trying to learn about God. If we are created in God's image, shouldn't we want to understand the complete image of God presented in the Bible?

If we aspire to discover God, we must spend most of our time in the Old Testament because that is where God directly appears. In the New Testament, God is not a character who speaks and acts in the narrative like he does in the Old Testament. In the Gospels, Jesus speaks about God, as do Paul and the writers of the other New Testament books, and those passages are obviously important. But, it's one thing to talk about God and another thing for God to be revealed as a character in a story. When God acts, we should watch carefully; and when God speaks, we should listen.

But, you say, Jesus is God. Yes, the Gospel of John claims that Jesus is God incarnate — God in the flesh. The question then becomes, Jesus is an incarnation of which God? Obviously the answer is the Jewish God, the God of the Old Testament — not Hindu gods, or Norse gods, or Native American gods. Jesus is an incarnation of the God we meet in the Old Testament. Shouldn't we then do our best to study that God?

It is commonly observed that God in the New Testament — either in the person of Jesus or as he is described — is a God of love and mercy, and that the God of the Old Testament is a God of vengeance and wrath. A *New Yorker* cartoon, for example, depicts a man approaching God's office and asking the angel at the front desk, "Is he the God of the Old Testament or the God of the New Testament today?" Similarly, a scene in the *The Simpsons* features Homer looking at a hologram which shows a mean, fiery God, and then, when tilted, reveals a smiling, friendly image. Homer tilts the hologram back and forth saying, "Vengeful God, loving God" and later notes, "God is a God of love, but also of great anger and wrath."

God's penchant for "anger and wrath" is no secret. But what is a secret — or is kept a secret from most believers — is that the God of the Old Testament is not merely a God of justice, wrath, and vengeance, not a God who simply punishes violently when people break his commandments, as Homer observes. Rather, he is portrayed as cruel, vindictive, childish, petulant, misogynistic, egotistical, genocidal, and maniacal. Yes, that's a brutally raw list of adjectives. But it does not take a scholarly, intellectual analysis to see this. College students (and "college" should not be confused with "scholarly" and "intellectual") routinely make these sorts of observations when asked to read and describe the portrayal of God. No, it does not take an academic degree or specialized training. But it does take a willingness to read what is written and to be candid about what we find.

If we open the Bible with pre-conceived, firmly-established beliefs about the nature of God, and refuse to reconsider those beliefs, then we might as well not examine the Scripture at all. If we are committed, for instance, to the idea that God is absolutely perfect, holy, and just, then no matter what God says or does in the text, we will force it to fit with those beliefs. The human mind is very good at seeing what it wants to see (just listen to talk radio) in order to explain away what it cannot digest.

Shouldn't we, instead, read the Bible first, and then draw conclusions about the character of God, rather than determining what we think about God and then forcing the Bible to fit those ideas? Furthermore, from where are we getting those pre-determined notions about God, if not from the Bible? Do we merely believe what our pastors, priests, teachers, and parents have told us? And from where are they getting their ideas? Doesn't it seem more appropriate to begin with — or at least include somewhere — an authentic, honest reading of Scripture to learn about God?

Let's try this little experiment. Consider the following passage about an ancient deity named Dusan and his interactions with the people who worship him, the people of Lith (Lithites).

Dusan declared concerning his own people the Lithites: "I will make your weapons useless against the king of Nolsum who is outside your walls attacking you. In fact, I will bring your enemies right into the heart of this city. I myself, Dusan, will fight against you with a strong hand and a powerful arm, for I am very angry. You have made me furious! I will send a terrible pestilence upon this city, and both people and animals will die. And after that I will hand over your king and everyone else in the city who survives the plagues of disease, war, and famine to King Ramiro of Nolsum. He will slaughter them and show them no mercy, pity, or compassion."

Dusan continued: "You people have acted more perversely than your neighbors and have refused to obey my decrees and laws. Therefore, I myself, Dusan, am now your enemy. I will punish you publicly while all the nations watch. Because of your detestable idols, I will punish you like I have never punished anyone before or ever will again. Parents will eat their own children, and children will eat their parents. I will punish you and scatter to the winds the few who survive.

"As surely as I live," says Dusan, "I will cut you off entirely. I will show you no pity at all because you have profaned my temple with your disgusting and detestable acts. A third of your people will die in the city from disease and famine. A third of them will be slaughtered by the enemy outside the city walls. And I will scatter a third to the winds, chasing them with my sword. Then at last my anger will be spent, and I will be satisfied. And when my fury has subsided, all Lith will know that I, Dusan, have spoken to them in my jealous anger.

"So I will turn you into a mockery in the eyes of the surrounding nations. You will become an object of taunting and horror. You will be a warning to all the nations around you. They will see what happens when Dusan punishes a nation in anger and rebukes it.

"I will send deadly arrows of famine to destroy you. The famine will become more and more severe until every crumb of food is gone. Furthermore, wild animals will attack you and rob you of your children. Disease and war will ravage your land, and I will bring the sword against you. I, Dusan, have spoken.

So what is your reaction to Dusan? What adjectives would you use to describe him? It seems to me that Dusan is not a nice guy. He declares his intentions to destroy and degrade and humiliate his own people. What kind of "good" deity says and does such things?

I suspect you have figured out what is going on here. The answer is: Your God, and my God. Ezekiel 5 says so. Changing the names simply de-familiarizes the text; it helps us think about it objectively. Surely we can agree that an honest and unbiased study of God's nature and character is a good and worthwhile undertaking. Doing so requires that we read passages such as Ezekiel 5, which are much harder to stomach than the more toothsome texts such as the popular Jeremiah 29:11, "For I know the plans that I have for you says the Lord, plans to prosper you and not to harm you, plans to give you a hope and a future." Imagine if church marquees put up quotes from Ezekiel 5 instead of Jeremiah 29.

So where are these passages (besides Ezekiel 5) that preachers never talk about? Actually, there are a lot of them. Too many in fact too discuss here. So before we start, let's indicate which passages we will not address, though they are numerous and problematic.

God makes a covenant with the people of Israel and promises to bless them if they obey his commands and to curse them if they do not. Reading the curse passages such as Deuteronomy 28 can be frightening, especially verses like 28:63 where God claims that he will enjoy bringing ruin and destruction on his people if they violate his word. The Israelites, as you probably know, do frequently break the covenant by worshiping other deities, thereby rousing God's ire and jealousy. In such cases, God's punishment could be seen as justified and fair, no matter how harsh it might appear. So for passages like Ezekiel 5 and a host of others — Exodus 19, Numbers 16, 1 Samuel 6, 2 Kings 1, and Jeremiah 21, to name a few — we will give God the benefit of the doubt and let him off the hook. That still leaves plenty to talk about. Let that sink in for a minute: Ezekiel 5 is actually one of the more defensible portrayals of God!

As we begin, one word of reminder: Read the texts for yourself. I repeat: Read the texts for yourself. Stop and picture clearly in your mind what is being described. Mull it over. Envision it. Many times it may leave a bad taste in your mouth. But it is necessary.

DID GOD SAY HE WAS SORRY?

We don't have to go very far into the Bible before we encounter challenging images of God. Genesis 6-8 features the well-known story of Noah and the flood. Frankly, I am not sure why this one is so popular. Maybe it's because most of us enjoy a nice summer day on the boat. Perhaps we tell it to our children because they like stories about animals. But when we stop and think about it, this is a horrific, brutally violent, and truly heart-breaking tale.

God "repents" that he made humankind and announces his decision to destroy the whole earth with a flood—a world he himself has just created. Yes, we are only six chapters into the Bible and God is already repenting. Some translations say "regret" instead of "repent" as a way to reduce the theological difficulty. But the fact of the matter is that it is the exact same Hebrew word which is always translated "repent" when it refers to people. But no matter. Either way God wishes that he had not created the world. And not just in an "aw-shucks" kind of way. No, he's really upset and angry with the way things have turned out. So mad is God that he aims to destroy the whole world. And that is putting it nicely, impersonally, generally. Let's say it specifically how God does: "I will wipe from the face of the earth the human race that I have created—and with them the animals, the birds, and the creatures of the earth that move along the ground." To put it succinctly and pointedly, God declares, "I will kill every person and animal on the planet."

Truthfully, how do we miss this? How do we manage to read right over such a declaration by God Almighty and not pause to grapple with it? This is not some obscure passage tucked away in Habakkuk. It's one of the most familiar stories in Scripture, and it begins with God, our God, announcing that he is so disgusted with humankind that he intends to kill them all, except for one man and his family. To be sure, there is a reason: the people are wicked and their every inclination and thought is evil. It is certainly nice to know there is a method to God's madness, so to speak. But that does not erase the theological problems; three questions remain, at least that I can think of—you may have more.

One, even though God has a stated reason for the annihilation, our natural human sensibilities are uncomfortable with God's actions. To illustrate, let me ask this question: How many days does Noah preach to the people, trying to convince then to repent or else perish in the flood? . . . . . . Answer: zero. He does not preach. Most children's Bibles and church retellings add that element into the story. Thus, you probably thought it was in the biblical account, but it's not. So why do they add it? Because we feel better — I guess — imagining that the wicked folks who drown were the ones laughing and poking fun at Noah as he pleaded with them to change their ways. It justifies their demise. In the biblical version, God declares humankind to be wicked; then he executes them. There is no opportunity to repent; there are no second chances; there is no forgiveness. That's unsettling.

Two, even if we grant God that all humans were depraved, we still must ask about the children? How can a baby be wicked? How can a newborn be held morally accountable? How could an infant deserve to die? Think of the toddlers washed away in the swelling waters. It's gut-wrenching. Remarkably, the Bible itself prompts us to ask this question. Just a few chapters later, in Genesis 18, is the narrative of Sodom and Gomorrah, which we discussed in the Introduction. In that story, when God apprises Abraham of his intention to incinerate Sodom, Abraham objects on moral grounds, arguing that if there are righteous people living in the city, then God should not destroy it. God agrees. We, then, can extend and apply Abraham's reasoning to the flood story by pointing out that infants and children cannot justifiably deserve to be killed. It is immoral and unfair for God to obliterate indiscriminately — not distinguishing between the guilty and the innocent. Again, that's what Abraham says, not me.

Third, why kill the animals? How can they be deemed wicked? The animals, notably, are not collateral damage. God makes it perfectly clear that he intends to wipe them out too in the flood (Genesis 6:7). I am not sure if the fish drowned, but the question remains. God, it seems, was not a charter member of PETA.

It does not matter, by the way, for the purpose of this discussion, whether or not the flood story, or any other Old Testament text, is historically accurate. It is irrelevant if the flood really happened. That is an entirely separate question. What matters is the theology of the text—what the Bible says about God. What it depicts here is a God who drowns men, women, boys, girls, toddlers, babies, puppies, kittens, and cubs. And he shows absolutely no remorse for doing so. At the end, God vows not to destroy the world again, but he never expresses an inkling of sorrow for wreaking such devastation. The church's censored version waters down, if you will, the story's conclusion as well. We like to picture Noah getting off the ark onto plush green grass with a beautiful rainbow overhead. But more realistically, more honestly, imagine the utter carnage he would have encountered: corpses of animals and humans everywhere. It'd be gruesome. It's truly amazing that this sad and profoundly disturbing story is a Sunday school favorite.

WHY DIDN'T PHARAOH LET THE PEOPLE GO?

There are certainly other stories in Genesis which we could sample (such as those in chapters 11, 20, and 22—you can put those in your to-go box and try them on your own later), but let's move on to three different passages in the book of Exodus. As you perhaps recall, the people of Israel are in slavery in Egypt. God hears their cries of oppression and plans to liberate them. He appears to Moses in the famous burning bush and charges him with the task of confronting Pharaoh and leading the Israelites out of Egypt—hence the title of the book, "Exodus."

Here is where we stop to consider our first scene. Exodus 4:24-26 is one of the oddest passages in Scripture. Moses, his wife Zipporah, and their son are on their way back to Egypt to carry out God's commands when we read this: "On the way, at a place where they spent the night, the Lord met him and tried to kill him. But Zipporah took a flint knife and cut off her son's foreskin, and touched Moses' feet with it. 'Surely you are a bridegroom of blood to me,' she said. So The Lord let him alone."

You should probably have the deer-in-the-headlights look on your face right now. What on earth is going on here? I'll tell you the answer: I have no clue whatsoever, and neither does anyone else. The whole scene has utterly baffled commentators.

It is unclear whether God is trying to kill Moses or Moses' son; but either way, God is out to kill someone. It's either the man he has just chosen to emancipate his people or an innocent child, who after the impromptu midnight circumcision is probably not so innocent anymore. Talk about a nightmare for that kid! This seemingly unprovoked divine assault is very strange to say the least. Perhaps God is upset that Moses has not circumcised his son—though that's not clear from the text. Even so, it seems rather belligerent to kill Moses or the boy on that account.

Apparently, though, and fortunately, Zipporah knew what was going on and was able to save her family, though no one has any idea of the significance of her words and actions — touching her son's foreskin to Moses' feet and uttering something about a bridegroom of blood. Incidentally, if you are looking for smart, strong women in the Bible, Zipporah should probably be at the top of your list as she is the only woman who fights off an attack by God (I wanted to name my daughter Zipporah — figured we'd call her Zippy — but it was vetoed). At any rate, this story depicts an unpredictable and mysterious deity, to put it mildly, who might show up in the middle of the night and attempt to slay you (or your son) for no obvious reason. Thus, it's always a good idea, as Zipporah knew, to have your flint knife handy.

There's a good chance you have never even heard this story — it's easy enough to skip it in church. But I suspect that you know generally how things go after that. Moses arrives in Egypt and he and his brother Aaron confront Pharaoh and demand the release of the Israelites. Pharaoh refuses and so God sends the ten plagues on the Egyptians. Then the Israelites escape into the wilderness and Pharaoh dispatches his army to pursue them. God miraculously splits the Red Sea and the Israelites cross safely on dry ground. When the Egyptians chase after them into the seabed, the walls of water crash down on them and they drown.

On the one hand, this is a wonderful story of God's concern and compassion for the alienated, oppressed Israelites. But, on the other hand, when we read the account carefully and in its entirety, we discover some deeply disconcerting facets of God.

First, the plagues. All of them are seemingly cruel, but, one could argue, the first nine are just annoying inconveniences (flies, gnats, frogs, hail, darkness, etc.). The tenth one, however, is a totally different scenario. God strikes dead the firstborn in every house throughout Egypt. Stop and think about that for a moment. That's a lot of dead people. Imagine the cries of anguish and grief and suffering as countless Egyptian parents who have nothing whatsoever to do with Pharaoh's refusal to free the Israelites mourn for their deceased children. Picture the funerals and mass graves. As in the flood story, God is not working on a case-by-case basis. If you are an Egyptian, your oldest child dies. Period.

Secondly, why didn't Pharaoh let the people go? This is not a joke. Answer: God himself hardens Pharaoh's heart. God manipulates Pharaoh, so that he will *not* cooperate. The text does not say this one time in passing; on the contrary, it states this repeatedly so it's difficult to miss (7:3; 9:15-16; 10:1-2, 27; 11:10; 14:1-4; 14:17-18). Next question: Why does God harden Pharaoh's heart? Answer: So that he can show Pharaoh and the Egyptians that they should love God instead of resist God — so that he can lovingly demonstrate to them the error of their ways and gently lead them to the truth. . . . Just joking. The answer is so that God can send the plagues, which will prove to the Egyptians that God is the biggest, baddest deity there is. I am serious. Read Exodus 4:21-23 and 7:3-5 where God makes it abundantly clear that his plan from the very beginning is to harden Pharaoh's heart so that God can destroy all the firstborn in Egypt. God turns Pharaoh into a puppet for the express purpose of destroying thousands of Egyptians so that the Egyptians "will know that I am the Lord." Incredibly, even after the Israelites have escaped, God continues to manipulate the Egyptians so that he can flex his muscles and demolish them. In Exodus 14:1-4 God commands the Israelites to act as if they are lost and confused in the wilderness in order to bate the Egyptians into chasing them, so that God can "gain glory for myself over Pharaoh" and so that the "Egyptians will know that I am the Lord" when they drown in the Red Sea.

We could get into a long discussion about free will versus predestination and so forth. But come on, let's admit that quite straightforwardly God speaks and acts in very unappealing ways here. It is difficult to conclude that God's sole and primary objective is to free the enslaved Israelites. If that were the case, he could have softened Pharaoh's heart so that he allowed the Israelites to leave peacefully, or he could have seemingly devised some other less violent means of emancipation. Surely God could have saved the Israelites without killing all the first born in Egypt and drowning the entire army. He willfully chose not to because he wanted, at least in part, to show the Egyptians who was boss. And he did so by destroying tens of thousands of them.

Alright let's move on (though that won't be so easy for Egyptian mothers). After the Israelites cross the Red Sea, they head to Mount Sinai where God gives them a lengthy set of laws by which to live; these laws fill up most of the books of Exodus, Leviticus, and Numbers. So let's go through them one by one . . . No, not really. It is important, though, to underscore the simple fact that, according to the biblical text, God gives these laws to Moses; they are not written and promulgated by humans, the Israelites. They are the words of God. Thus they say something about the nature and character of God.

Christians like to hold up the Ten Commandments, for example, as a set of laws that reflect a good, ethical, moral, righteous deity. But then we completely ignore the less tasteful mandates. To be sure, the Old Testament laws are a weird mix. Alongside the troubling laws are commands to show compassion to widows, orphans, aliens, and the poor. Wonderfully benevolent commands are followed by ones we shrug off as irrelevant. There is no better example of such a peculiar juxtaposition than Leviticus 19:18 and 19. The former says, "Love your neighbor as yourself" while the latter forbids wearing garments made of two different kinds of thread. We esteem verse 18 as exemplary of the God we worship, but then disregard his very next instruction. Can't we love our neighbor while wearing a cotton-polyester blend?

To be consistent, all of the legal material in the Old Testament should be considered a reflection of the lawgiver, God. Unfortunately, much of it does not match our values or our image of who God is. When we read through the laws, we discover profoundly disturbing ones that do not respect human life as we do. For example, the death penalty is required for having sex with an animal, cursing your parents, committing adultery, breaking the Sabbath, being a recalcitrant and disobedient child, and kidnapping, just to name a few. For the record, I would have been executed, though no need to say for which crime(s). I am sure you would have been too.

Women certainly are not treated fairly by the laws. They are penalized every month by menstruation, which makes them unclean. Daughters can be sold as slaves (Exodus 21:7), and men are permitted to take multiple wives, though women are not permitted multiple husbands, of course (which is probably a blessing). If a woman is raped in a city, as opposed to the open country, she is automatically considered a willing participant because it is assumed that she did not cry for help, in which case she would have been heard (Deuteronomy 22:25-27). Furthermore, the female victim was forced to marry her rapist (Deuteronomy 22:28-29). God also sanctioned the rape of foreign women taken in battle (Numbers 31:15-18).

Wouldn't we agree that the abuse of women is morally and ethically wrong in every context, in every time and place? We cannot say, "Well, God allowed that back then, but it's not okay now." Tell that to the twelve-year-old Israelite girl who was raped in a town and couldn't scream loud enough.

Then there are slaves. It's bad enough that God allowed the Israelites to have slaves, but at least the slaves could be treated decently. No such luck. In Exodus 21:20-21, just a page after the famous Ten Commandments, we read this horrifying law: "When a slave owner strikes a male or female slave with a rod and the slave dies immediately, the owner shall be punished. But if the slave survives a day or two, there is no punishment; for the slave is the owner's property." That's raw stuff. According to Scripture, God gave a law stating that it is perfectly legal to beat your slave to death, as long as he or she doesn't die on the spot. If the slave expires a couple of days later because of the beating, there is no penalty. (A few modern translations try to soften the blow of this verse, but they cannot expunge the brutality of it.)

Close your eyes and picture a young female slave being brutally and repeatedly clubbed by her master; she sustains several broken bones and is so bloody and bruised that she can barely make it back to the house, but she does. Four days later, her frail and shattered body can no longer sustain her. She dies. God's verdict on the master: Innocent.

These laws form the basis of the covenant relationship between God and the Israelites. Thus, they are absolutely central and crucial for understanding the nature of God in the Old Testament. They cannot be ignored, but of course they are. We've heard preachers attempt to circumvent the issue with barbequed statements like these: (a) God gave those laws to Israelites, not Christians. (b) God did not really say those things, only the Israelites did. (c) We should learn from the principles of the laws, not the specifics. (d) The New covenant obviates the Old one. (e) Today we must obey only the moral laws, not the ceremonial ones. And the list goes on.

But observe what each of these responses is doing. They are addressing the question of how Christians should understand the Jewish laws or whether or not the laws apply to Christians today. But that is not the issue! The issue is not the laws, it's the lawgiver. Of course we don't follow the specific laws today. But we do claim to follow the lawgiver, God. That's the problem.

The bottom line, then, is this: According to Scripture, the God we worship instituted this law code. God authorized every law we read in the Old Testament, and laws reflect the values and character of the lawgiver. Furthermore, if we wish to appeal to the New Testament, Jesus declared that he came not to abolish the law, but to fulfill it; he said that not one stroke or letter of the law would ever disappear and he taught people that they should adhere to the laws (as we will see in the next course). Jesus himself, quite clearly, affirmed the Old Testament laws, and with them the nature of the deity who authored them.

HOW COULD GOD DO *THAT?*

After giving the laws—all 613 of them—to the Israelites, God leads his people to the Promised Land. Way back in Genesis 12, God had vowed to Abraham that he would give his descendants this plot of ground on which to live, the land of Israel. Now in the book of Joshua, God fulfills that oath. The stories in Joshua, then, are vital to the broader Old Testament narrative; they are not some inconsequential, isolated sidebars. No, they represent the long awaited completion of the promise to Abraham.

Battle stories, I suppose, are never pretty. As they say, war is hell. And the book of Joshua certainly lives up to that. The first battle as the Israelites storm the land is at Jericho. The Israelites send out two spies to scout the area. Of all the places they could have gone, they end up at Rahab the prostitute's house—how convenient for two guys doing out-of-town business. Rahab, whose name means "wide" (wink wink), protects the men and helps them escape. You perhaps know the rest of the story, for it's a Sunday school favorite. The Israelites march around the city seven times— apparently the spies weren't able to gather any good information at Rahab's place—and then God causes the walls of Jericho to collapse. Hurray. What happens next, though, you probably aren't aware of, for obvious reasons. At God's command, the Israelites kill everyone in Jericho. The text reads: Then they "devoted to destruction by the edge of the sword every living being in the city, both men and women, young and old, oxen, sheep, and donkeys" (6:21). Only

Rahab is saved. Everyone else is slaughtered. Everyone. That's everyone.

Pause to reflect on the massive carnage in Jericho. Defenseless women, children, and babies screaming as the Israelites slash them to pieces. The popularity of this story is a tribute to the church's selective reading of Scripture. We cheer the collapse of the walls, but preachers never invite us to consider the fact that God commands — and the Israelites carry out — a mass murder of Jericho's citizens. And it's not because the people of Jericho were wicked and evil; it's because they were non-Israelites who were living in the land that God gave to Abraham's family. God, it should be underscored, is not defending his people from violent aggressors. The Israelites are the ones invading the land and butchering every man, woman, child, and animal.

Joshua 10:28-43 is a summary of the kings and cities that the Israelites defeat as they violently seize control of the Promised Land. (For the nerdy historians in the group, remember that whether or not this ever happened is irrelevant for our purposes. We are doing theology here.) In each instance Joshua and the Israelites "left no one remaining, but utterly destroyed all that breathed, as the Lord God of Israel commanded." Everyone in every city. This is unpalatable enough, but God's stated reason for doing so is even harder to swallow. It's frighteningly reminiscent of Exodus: "There was not a town that made peace with the Israelites, except the Hivites, the inhabitants of Gibeon. All were taken in battle. For it was the Lord's doing to harden their hearts so that they would come against Israel in battle, in order that they might be utterly destroyed, and might receive no mercy, but be exterminated, just as the Lord had commanded Moses" (Joshua 11:20). Gasp. Wince. Cringe. God orchestrates the whole thing precisely so that the native inhabitants will be slaughtered! There is no mercy, only extermination. God does not instruct the Israelites to try to make peace or to convert the people residing in the land; rather he mandates their complete annihilation. The genocide of the Canaanites is not an unfortunate result of a failed treaty or irreconcilable religious differences. No. It is the express plan of God. He wants them to be exterminated. God himself says so. That is what the biblical text says.

Again, let's put a face on the suffering. Envision each person, each little boy and girl and baby, in these towns being impaled by Israelite swords, with God standing by approving the massacre. Picture the bloody and ghastly scene. Then we must face the fact that according to our Scripture, that was the design and desire of our God.

DOES GOD ACCEPT CHILD SACRIFICE?

So far we have sampled some fairly well-known texts, though I suspect they taste a bit different ungreased. The remainder of this course, however, features morsels that you may not have previously encountered (save one). These passages, of course, are no less important—they too are every bit as much a part of the Bible.

We skipped over Genesis 22, the famous account of God "testing" Abraham by telling him to sacrifice his son Isaac (a story I always reference when students complain about the difficulty of my tests). Without doubt, that is a profoundly disquieting text, but it's chockfull of complex issues, so we set it aside. And plus, God ultimately stops Abraham. The story in Judges 11 returns us again to the topic of God and child sacrifice, but this time the ending isn't so happy.

Here the warrior Jephthah makes a vow to God that if God will grant him victory in battle, he will sacrifice the first thing that comes out of his house when he returns. Who knows what Jephthah was thinking when he said this — maybe he figured it would be some animal, or perhaps his mother-in-law. So Jephthah goes to war and is victorious. When he rides home triumphantly, his daughter, his only child, comes hurrying out to greet him. Jephthah is utterly distraught, but amazingly, the girl encourages him to keep his word. She asks for a few months to lament with her girl-friends, which Jephthah grants. Then he burns his daughter to death as a sacrifice to God.

The scenario, then, is this: God hears Jephthah's oath, grants him victory, and takes no action to stop the immolation of the nameless girl. Is God tacitly accepting her burnt body as an offering? Does he want the young woman to be slaughtered? The lack of divine intervention stands in striking contrast to the Abraham and Isaac story. If God is disgusted with Jephthah's sacrifice, why not stop it? Or at least express disdain? Or God could have withheld victory in the first place. There are numerous things God could have said or done to indicate his disapproval of the sacrifice. But there is nothing, only silence. Maybe God allowed Jephthah to go through with it as a punishment for his rash oath, but that seems awfully insensitive to the plight of the poor girl. Imagine her body, the knife, the flames.

We could probably dismiss the whole idea of God receiving human sacrifice were it not for one really troubling text in Ezekiel. Here is what God says in little-known Ezekiel 20:25-26, a passage in which God is reviewing the history of his relationship with Israel: "I also gave them statutes that were not good and laws they could not live by; I defiled them through their gifts — their sacrificing every firstborn — in order that I might horrify them so that they would know that I am the Lord." Here God declares that he gave his people bad laws, including requiring them to sacrifice their children, precisely so that the people would be aghast and dismayed. Not only that, but he does so in order to enhance his own reputation ("so they would know that I am the Lord"). That's what the text says. I am simply reading my Bible.

Whether or not the Israelites actually practiced child sacrifice to the Lord is debated among scholars. The answer does not matter for our purposes. What matters is that in this story God does not stop Jephthah from offering his little girl as a burnt offering. Perhaps we should observe a moment of silence for this otherwise unknown maiden.

WHY DID GOD DRIVE SAUL CRAZY?

After they had been in the Promised Land for a while, the people of Israel decide they wanted a king like the nations around them. This displeases God who felt it was a rejection of his leadership (1 Samuel 8). Nonetheless, he begrudgingly grants them one in the form of King Saul. Saul's kingship, however, is not a happy one, as God seems to have it out for him from the very beginning. In fact, God literally drives Saul crazy.

God's relationship with Saul in 1 Samuel is complex and disturbing on a number of levels. But we will keep it simple and focus on only one aspect, only one verse as it were. One verse can say a lot; but be sure to read it in context. Don't trust me. After God has rejected Saul as king for failing to exterminate the Amalekites (1 Samuel 15, an alarming story in itself), God anoints David as the future king of Israel and the spirit of the Lord is transferred from Saul to David (16:13-14). God, as he himself says, withdrew his love from Saul and gave it to David (2 Samuel 7:15). But that is not all: "The spirit of the Lord departed from Saul, and an evil spirit from the Lord tormented him (1 Samuel 16:14)." Now there's a cold, hard biblical phrase for us to ponder: "An evil spirit from the Lord." Yes, God sends an evil spirit to persecute Saul, which it does by driving him insane, as can be seen in the remainder of 1 Samuel where Saul goes crazy and winds up committing suicide. Who or what the spirit is and how it is evil are not spelled out for us. But we know its evil — it's the common, standard word always rendered "evil" — there's nothing tricky going on with translation. And we know it's from God. Maybe it's the Holy Spirit's wicked twin.

Evil from God. Evil to torment his chosen king — not some bad guy. Evil to drive him ultimately to death — not for some greater good. I wonder what Saul would think of the words to the old hymn, "God is so good. He's so good to me." This, incidentally, is not the only time that we see God as the genesis of evil. In addition to the book of Job, discussed below, check out Isaiah 45:7, Amos 3:6, and Micah 1:12. Be sure to read these verses in context, but it's evident that God claims that he causes "evil" — though some translations render the Hebrew word (the same one used here with Saul) as "disaster" or "woe" in these verses.

WHY WOULD GOD KILL THE BABY?

King David follows King Saul. He has much better luck with God. He is even described repeatedly as a "man after

God's own heart," which is interesting since, as you may be aware, David had plenty of foibles.

One such story which illustrates David's faults is his affair with Bathsheba. You probably know it since we tend to like stories about powerful men, beautiful women, sex, and murder. Plus, preachers like to tell this one because it always makes us feel better about ourselves knowing that a guy this wicked is still loved by God. It's sort of like watching the *Jerry Springer Show*: my life may be bad, but it's not *this* bad. Just in case you don't know the tale, here it is, Tarzan-style: David King. King see beautiful woman bathing. King want woman. Woman married. King still get woman. King have sex with woman. Woman get pregnant. King kill husband. Beautiful woman become King's wife. Have baby.

I am guessing that is about as much as you know from church. What happens next is not quite as fun. Tarzan would finish it this way: God mad. God kill baby.

Tarzan is right. The Lord sends the prophet Nathan to confront David and announce the punishment. Among other things, the penalty includes the death of Bathsheba's child. Second Samuel 12:15 reads: "The Lord struck the child . . . and it became very ill." David pleads for mercy, but to no avail, for "on the seventh day the child died" (12:18). Perhaps this falls into the "wages of sin is death" category, thus effectively exonerating God. But still, why kill the innocent child as punishment for David's failures? The child did not do anything. Note that God does not "allow" the child to become ill or "allow" the child to die. No, God purposely and intentionally strikes the child dead.

Another story featuring God and David is found in 2 Samuel 24, which we mentioned in the first course, but let's "count" it again. Here David takes a census; God is displeased and gives the king a choice of three forms of punishment: famine, warfare, or plague. I am sure David was pleased to have such good options. David chooses the plague, and God obliges by sending an angel who kills 70,000 Israelites. This scenario, by the way, sounds like many of the ones we have skipped over — God punishing his people for a sin by unleashing a deadly pestilence of some kind. This passage, however, is different in one major way. Verse 1 reads, "The anger of the Lord was kindled against Israel, and he incited David against them saying: Go count the people of Israel and Judah." The text does not tell us why God is angry. But more befuddling is why God would cause David to take a census, and then when David obeys, God sends a death angel to slay tens of thousands of otherwise innocent Israelites. David himself in verse 17 observes the unfairness of the plague in terms of the massive number of blameless dead. What kind of God kills 70,000 of his own people — stop and think about how many lost lives that is! — on account of a census that he himself prompted?

DID GOD LIE?

We move from the best king, David, to the worst king, Ahab. But we continue to find questionable images of our God. First Kings 22 is one weird text. Here King Ahab of Israel is seeking guidance from the prophets about whether he should go to war. That seems quite a righteous thing to do for a guy who has such a bad reputation. Four hundred of the prophets declare in the name of the Lord that Ahab will be victorious. One of them was even dancing around with a pair of iron horns saying, "This is how you will gore your enemy to death" (ancient prophets were cool — Ezekiel does the same type of thing). At the prompting of his ally, King Jehoshephat, Ahab consults one more seer, Micaiah, who always prophecies bad things about Ahab. This time, though, Micaiah declares, "Attack and be victorious, for God will give you victory." Evidently, however, Micaiah had a habit of being sarcastic, for Ahab says, "How many times do I have to tell you to give me only the truth?" Micaiah then responds, and I am paraphrasing here, "Yeah, just kidding. Your army will be defeated and you will die, sucker."

This is already weird enough, but it gets weirder. Micaiah then goes on to provide an explanation for the positive message of the 400 prophets. He reports having seen a vision of the heavenly court in which God asked, "Who will entice Ahab, so that he may go to war and perish?" One spirit proposes that he will "go out and become a lying spirit in the mouth of all his prophets." God approves the idea and commissions the spirit, which explains why all the prophets are forecasting success for Ahab.

Let's be sure we get this straight: Ahab desires to know what God wants him to do about the battle, so he consults the prophets. God intentionally deceives Ahab by sending a lying spirit into the mouths of the 400 prophets in hopes that Ahab will be misled, decide to go to war, and be killed. Not only does God dupe Ahab, but he does so using his own name — that is, the 400 prophesy in the name of the Lord (verses 7 and 11).

If God wore pants, they'd be on fire. How is this story to be aligned with the notion that God is truth?

IS GOD A GAMBLER?

The story of Job is commonly misrepresented in church, and for good reason. In the church's version, Job is the righteous man who remains faithful to God despite great suffering; it is a story of tremendous courage and hope. Unfortunately, once we read the book of Job, even just the first two chapters, the inspiration vanishes rather quickly.

God starts a conversation with Satan in which God notes that Job is a man of righteousness and integrity. Satan responds that Job is a good, faithful man because he is interested in obtaining blessings and wealth from God. Job, in other words, is faithful because he knows God will reward him. God doesn't agree. So the two make a wager, a friendly celestial bet. It's like God and Satan went to Vegas—only what happens here doesn't stay here. They agree to take away all of Job's blessings to see how he reacts. Then they will know who is right. Specifically, his children are killed and his possessions are destroyed. Job remains loyal to God. God wins the bet. But apparently the original wager was a parlay—you have to win twice to win the bet. So they do it again, this time inflicting Job with terrible physical suffering. Again Job does not turn away from God.

The central question jumps off the page: Why would God put one innocent man through such awful pain and misery—including the death of his children—just to prove a point to Satan? And let's be clear: God, not Satan, is responsible for the evil brought upon Job. The biblical text leaves no doubt about this fact. First, Job himself suspects that God is behind it when he says, "The Lord gave and the Lord has taken away" and "Shall we receive the good from the hand of God, and not receive the bad?" (1:21 and 2:10). Job knows that God, not Satan, has taken away and doled out the bad. Secondly, in 2:3 God himself admits to it when he says to Satan, "You incited me against Job, to destroy him for no reason." We cannot miss the import of this verse: God takes full responsibility for the tragedies brought upon Job and, moreover, admits that they had no purpose. God does not say to Satan: "Look what *you* did to him for no reason." He says: "You provoked *me* to destroy him." Satan carried out the deeds, but he is not the one who is ultimately responsible. Satan may have been the bullet that killed Job's family, but God pulled the trigger — and God admits to doing it for no reason whatsoever. According to God himself, it was not a test of Job's faith to make him stronger or any such interpretation we are likely to hear from the pulpit. Instead, Job's life was destroyed because of a purposeless, meaningless bet between God and Satan. God himself says so.

Furthermore, at the end of the book, just after God has restored Job, the same fact is stated by the narrator: Job's family and friends come "to show him sympathy and comfort for all the evil that the Lord had brought upon him" (42:11). Notice that it does not say, "for all the evil that *Satan* had inflicted on him" or "for all the evil that the Lord *allowed* to come upon him." No. God deliberately brings the evil — including the death of Job's children.

There is more. The bulk of the book of Job is a dialogue among Job and his friends. It is a rich, complex conversation in which Job struggles mightily to understand what has happened to him. He is deeply depressed to say the least (see, for example, Job 3). He confronts and questions God, maintains that he has done nothing to deserve such suffering, and accuses the deity of mercilessly tormenting him. He certainly is not Job the patient, wonderful man of faith who accepts his fate without murmuring and complaining — that's the mistaken church version. The biblical Job is broken, angry, and defiant.

God finally responds to Job in chapters 38-41 — a passage worth reading carefully in its entirety. A highly abridged version of God's speech goes like this: "Now I will question you and you will answer me. Do you know where the rain and snow comes from? Can you control the seas? Did you hang the stars in the sky? Does lightening obey you? Do you know when the mountain goat gives birth? Have you considered how amazing the ostrich is? Do you give the horse its strength? Can you tell the hawk how to soar? Can you tame the great beasts of the earth?"

It is a shocking and completely unexpected reply that can be interpreted variously, but God clearly does not answer any of Job's specific questions about his suffering. Perhaps we can imagine why, since that would entail revealing the bet with Satan. There is seemingly nothing kind and compassionate about the speech. God, after all, has wrecked Job's life, and yet God does nothing more than question him about the snow, the stars, and the ostrich. Picture the scene in your mind: Job is sitting on an ash heap, so emaciated from the physical illness God inflicted on him that he is nearly unrecognizable (2:7). After Job pours out his soul to God for chapter upon chapter, God shows up and asks him about ostriches. Ostriches! It's hardly an ideal model of pastoral counseling.

Sure, God restores Job at the end of the book. But is that supposed to make up for the ten original children for whose death God was responsible? Kids aren't toys that you just replace.

HAVE YOU STOPPED BEATING YOUR WIFE?

Prophets deliver God's message to the people of Israel. They are God's mouth piece, his spokesperson. What they say is the word of God; thus we should take it as a revelation of the character and nature of God. Preachers enjoy quoting the inspiring and uplifting passages from the prophets, such as Jeremiah 29:11, Ezekiel 37, Amos 5:24, and Micah 6:8. So let's take a look at a few that you will never hear about on Sunday morning — or ever.

The prophets Jeremiah, Ezekiel, and Hosea employ a marriage metaphor to describe the relationship between God and the Israelites. Specifically, God is depicted as the husband and Israel as the adulterous wife who has been unfaithful to God her husband by worshipping other deities. She has cheated on him with other gods, and God is irate. Yes, it is a metaphor, but that does not diminish the profoundly unsettling nature of God in these passages.

In Hosea 2, God expresses his anger toward his whoring wife. He declares that he will strip her naked and expose her like a newborn infant; he intends to kill her, taking no pity on her or her children. He will torment her, destroy her possessions, and humiliate her in front of her lovers. But then God declares that he will "allure" his wife, speak tenderly to her, and take her back as his bride. Here God is the jealous husband who goes on a violent rampage and then attempts to reunite with his wife. It sounds all too familiar for those who know anything about the psychology of abusive men.

In Ezekiel 16, God describes how he rescued Jerusalem, personified as a woman, when she was an unwanted infant, how he provided for her as she grew up, and how he eventually took her as his wife. But despite God's goodness, the girl Jerusalem turned into a brazen whore whose promiscuity God recounts in detail. Verses 35-43 outline in no uncertain terms the revenge that God will exact on her. Here is a condensed version: "Therefore, you whore, because of your lust, I will gather all your lovers and humiliate you by exposing you. I will turn you over to your lovers and they will strip you and leave you naked; they will bring a mob against you, stone you, and cut you into pieces. Thus I will stop you from being a whore; I will satisfy my fury against you. Because you have forgotten the days of your youth, but have enraged me, thus I have returned your deeds upon your head." And it gets worse.

Ezekiel 23 is the story of two sisters, Oholah, who represents the Israelite city of Samaria, and Oholibah, who is Jerusalem. Warning: this passage borders on the pornographic. Continue at your own risk.

The Lord tells how both sisters were whores from the beginning. They enjoyed having their breasts fondled when they were young. Oholah lusted after the Assyrian men and gods and bestowed her sexual favors on them. In response, the Lord turned her over to the Assyrians who abused her and killed her children. Even though Oholibah, Jerusalem, saw what had happened to her whoring sister, she nonetheless continued to flaunt her lustful ways. She chased after her men, the Babylonians, because they had large penises like horses and ejaculated like stallions. As a result, the Lord hands over Oholibah and her children to her enemies to be physically mutilated and killed. God is clear about his intentions to make the girl suffer as punishment for her promiscuity: "I will direct my anger against you, in order that they may deal with you in fury. They will cut off your nose and your ears...They will seize your sons and daughters...

They will strip you of your clothes…They will leave you naked and bare…Because you have forgotten me, and cast me behind your back, therefore you will bear the consequences of your lewdness and whorings" (verses 25-29).

These are graphic, deeply disturbing texts about God and his tumultuous relationship with his wife, his own chosen people. They are especially frightful images for readers who have experienced domestic violence. It's brutal enough for me to read them. I can only imagine how a battered wife would respond.

What would we say if a man treated his wife this way? To be sure, we may understand his anger and rage at being betrayed. But if he physically abused her, turned her over to be tortured and gang raped, and ultimately killed her, would we defend and justify those actions as moral? Should we then do so with God?

We have skipped over many Old Testament passages in which God violently punishes his people for disobeying him, so I suppose we could pass over these prophetic texts as well. But this marriage metaphor strikes a nerve. If God wants to destroy his own people with a plague because they have broken the covenant, okay, we can let it go. But when he proclaims that he will beat the daylights out of his wife, well, that is where we must draw the line.

DOES GOD LIKE BROWN NOSERS?

Just prior to meeting Jesus, the son of God — and God in the flesh — in the Gospels, the book of Malachi offers us two raw depictions of the God whom Jesus incarnates. These two portrayals are also particularly interesting because they appear immediately prior to one of the few places in the Old

Testament which talks about tithing, giving a percentage of your money to God. Thus you might get a sermon on Malachi 3 — especially since there God promises to pour out blessings if you give to God first — but we don't hear much about the God of Malachi 1 and 2.

Malachi 1 is a dialogue between God and the priests. God begins by declaring his love for Israel. The priests ask, "How have you loved us?" to which God answers, "I have loved Jacob, but I have hated Esau; I have made his hill country into a wasteland, and his heritage a desert for jackals." Jacob and Esau, you perhaps recall, were twin brothers in the stories in Genesis 25-34. Jacob's descendants became the people of Israel while Esau's descendants became the nation of Edom. So God, just to be clear, is declaring that he has loved and blessed the people of Jacob/Israel and he has hated and cursed the people of Esau/Edom.

In case you missed it here in Malachi, the New Testament says the exact same thing in Romans 9:11-13. That passage, believe it or not, goes a step further by stating that God hated Esau even before he was born. Wow. Can we say, then, that God loves everybody? Preachers, incidentally, are occasionally forced to deal with the Romans passage, for which they turn the burner on high and tell you that it "does not *really mean* that God hated Esau." I personally am uncomfortable with telling God that he does not mean what he says (though what he says may be mean). For me, when God says, "I hate Esau," I tend to interpret that to mean that God hates Esau.

Malachi 2 is also rather striking, or should we say stinky. As the conversation with the priests continues, God expresses his anger with them for disrespecting and dishonoring him by offering weak and sickly animals as sacrifices. God announces to his priests, "I will rebuke your offspring, and splatter manure on your faces, the manure of your offerings" (2:3). Oh my! God is really, really mad at his priests. You bring crappy animal sacrifices to me, God says, and I will take the animal crap and rub it all over your face. If you don't do enough brown nosing, I'll put the brown on your nose for you.

We may understand God's frustration, but his language is hardly reflective of a majestic, holy deity who deserves your money. From a minister's point of view, talking about tithing is more advantageous than preaching about poop.

Is God the Grim Reaper?

Finally, let's look at the image of the risen Christ in the New Testament book of Revelation. As we discussed earlier, God does not appear as a character in the New Testament in the same way that he does in the Old, but the Jesus of Revelation is depicted as a divine figure, so it's appropriate to consider these passages here. The image of the conquering Messiah in Revelation is quite different from the depiction of the earthly, human Jesus of the Gospels, whom we meet next. The book of Revelation has gotten a lot of press in recent years, namely, as a prophetic book which predicts events surrounding the end of the world; but lost in all that is the simple fact that the deified Christ we find in this book is a terribly fierce character.

It is true that he conquers and destroys the powers of evil, so perhaps that makes these bloodthirsty texts a bit more palatable, but still, the graphic violence is a disturbing contrast to the way in which preachers present Jesus.

The tension between traditional images of Jesus and those found in Revelation is articulated in a line from Homer, not the epic bard, but *The Simpsons* character. Homer, predicting the end of the world, shouts in the streets, "Jesus loves you! He's gonna kill you!" Indeed, reminiscent of the God of the Old Testament, the Jesus of Revelation is a powerful warrior who slays his enemies.

Revelation 1:12-16 features the one and only physical description of Christ in the entire New Testament. John, the writer of Revelation, says this: "I saw one like the Son of Man, clothed with a long robe, and with a golden sash across his chest. His head and hair were white as white wool, as white as snow. His eyes were like a flame of fire; his feet were like burnished bronze . . . and his voice was like the sound of many waters. In his right hand he held seven stars and from his mouth came a sharp two-edged sword, and his face was like the sun shining with full force." Not surprisingly, when we see paintings of Jesus, this is not it. Double-edged swords tend to scare people, especially little children.

There is no ambiguity about the purpose of the sword, as a second similar description of the Messiah makes clear in 19:11-21: "From his mouth comes a sharp sword with which to strike down the nations . . . . He will tread the wine press of the fury of the wrath of God the Almighty." Here Christ does not walk softly and carry a big stick. Instead he uses his stick to destroy his foes and then he stomps and tramples them to death just as one crushes grapes to make wine.

Then an angel calls the birds of earth to come feast on the carcasses of God's slaughtered enemies: "Come, gather for the great supper of God, to eat the flesh of kings, the flesh of captains, the flesh of the mighty, the flesh of the horses and their riders — the flesh of all, both free and slave, both small and great." This definitely is a very different kind of "Lord's supper" from the one we take in church. The passage then describes the destruction of the "beast" and the "false prophet" who are thrown into the lake of fire. The fate of those deceived by the false prophet is this: "And the rest were killed . . . by the sword that came from his mouth; and all the birds of the air were gorged with their flesh." Talk about truly raw texts. This is grisly stuff. God celebrates the slaughter not only of the beast and false prophet, but also of common folk — free and slave, small and great.

Likewise, chapter 14:14-21 features a description of "one like a Son of Man, with a golden crown on his head and a sharp sickle in his hand." He uses the sickle to reap the earth's harvest, which is thrown into the wine press, "and the wine press was trodden outside the city, and the blood flowed from the wine press, as high as a horse's bridle, for a distance of about two hundred miles." It's Jesus as the Grim Reaper — the sickle in his hand. This is rather different from Jesus' teaching in the Sermon on the Mount where he says, for example, "Turn the other cheek" and "Love your enemies and pray for those who persecute you." Homer Simpson was right: God is gonna kill you — if you aren't on his side.

These images of the deified Christ in Revelation illustrate the problems of drawing a simple dichotomy between a wrathful, vengeful God of the Old Testament and a loving, merciful one in the New Testament. The image of the Messiah in Revelation is an all too accurate incarnation of the God of the Old Testament. It is remarkable that these are the final pictures of the divine Christ in the Bible. If we were reading the Scripture straight through, we might have forgotten about the disturbing images of God back in the Old Testament, but Revelation serves as a jolting reminder. Indeed, from the flood story at the beginning of Genesis to the culmination of the grand narrative in Revelation, the biblical God is not the God we've met in church.

RAW REFLECTIONS

Scripture may not be the only place where God is revealed to us, but surely it is the primary one in our tradition. Thus, we must take the Bible — all of it — as fundamental revelation about our God. As honest Christians, we cannot say that we don't understand these troubling texts. No. We do understand them. We just don't find them palatable. How can we claim to comprehend the Bible when it says, "God is love," but then when God appears as deceptive, evil, and cruel, we say, "No, God is not really those things." Or we throw up our hands and say, "There are some things we can never grasp." Let's be real. Like Job says, we must take the good with the bad.

We, of course, have not focused on the "God is love" passages; to be sure, God is positively portrayed in many places in Scripture. But we already know about those. Those are the easy texts. What about the tough ones? They too are part of God's Word. How are we to digest them? What are we supposed to do and think now that we've met God uncensored? Two reflections come to mind, the first indispensable, the second dispensable.

First, to undertake the process of wrestling with God is to engage in a meaningful relationship with God. It's what brings us closer to God. It's how we love God. Struggling with God is not a means to an end; it is an end itself. When we are willing to wrestle with the unexpurgated God of our Scripture, we are loving God with our mind, as Jesus enjoined us. We are exercising our God-given and God-ordained abilities to think and reason. We are developing our faith like Abraham, Jacob, and the host of other biblical characters who engage God with their moral faculties, who question and challenge the Almighty. God gave us a mind so we can relate to God. If we do not analyze, criticize, and question, then we are mindless robots following God. The Bible does not call us to be mindless robots — in fact, there is not even one robot in the Bible.

If we are not encouraged to use our God-given intellect to learn about God, then we are being fed a fabricated faith, a faith that is antithetical to our heritage. Deeply embedded in our tradition is the belief that when we dare to strive with God, as opposed to passively submit, we come closer to God. Thus, the process of dealing with the God of Scripture deepens and strengthens our relationship with God.

If we ignore or reject or explain away the tasteless portrayals of our God, and accept only what we find agreeable, then we are the ones who are creating God. Scripture becomes unnecessary and God is nothing more than a projection of our own ideals. As the creator of God, we essentially become God. The world revolves around us. By contrast, if we allow Scripture to reveal God to us, then God becomes a separate entity, distinct from us, outside of us — or as philosophers like to say, God becomes truly Other. God then becomes an independent being whom we are free to love with our minds, rather than a being we have created with our minds. When we are able to love God as Other, we are able to love other people, who, of course, are also outside of ourselves.

For us to truly experience God as a being separate from our own hopes and expectations, distinct from how we want God to be, we must read the Scripture with a sense of honesty, objectivity, and integrity. Akin to our exercise with Dusan at the beginning of this course, an Israeli psychologist once did an experiment in which he gave one group of Jewish children the stories of genocide found in the book of Joshua. Most of them said that the characters acted in moral and justifiable ways. He gave another group of Jewish children the same stories but with the names changed to Chinese ones; nearly all of these children judged the actions unethical. Same exact text, but different responses because one group recognized it as part of their Scripture and the other group did not. It's okay when our God is killing innocent people, but not okay when your God does. It is surely part of human nature not to see one's own Scripture and beliefs objectively. But it's also a uniquely human capacity — the part of our nature that God gave to us and not the animals — to see ourselves as others see us, to see things from different points of view. And in this case, to see our God as others may see him.

If all the texts we have discussed in this course were not in the Bible, but instead were tales about Roman or Greek gods, or part of Native American mythology, what would we say about the deity? How would we evaluate his character? Would we deem him worthy of love, worship, and respect? If we refuse to make candid and impartial responses to questions such as these, we effectively eliminate any space for conversation, for meaningful religious dialogue. There can be no reasonable discussion with others. When we cannot talk to other people, when we cannot engage them as independent beings with minds of their own, then we cannot love them. But when we do love God with our mind — openly, honestly, objectively — we are able to live out the second greatest command: Love your neighbor as yourself. In short, the process of wrestling with God is an expression of our love for God and neighbor.

My second reflection is totally expendable. These are merely my thoughts on how I wrestle with the unfiltered God of Scripture. They may be very different from your striving, which is perfectly great. But I thought you might like to know what the waiter thinks about the menu.

For me, the paradoxical God of Scripture — kind and cruel, good and genocidal, present and absent — is the true nature of the God of the universe. God is not all good, powerful, holy, and loving; he's partly those things and partly their opposite. Following certain Christian theologians — nothing I ever say or think is original — I would suggest that God evolves and changes over time as he relates to his creation. God is in the process of learning and growing, just as we are. God, as is true of all living beings, is open and mutable, as in changeable (not "able to be muted," as on your TV remote). God isn't in complete control (he may not even have the remote). God isn't perfect. God doesn't know the future. And sometimes God doesn't bother to relate to his creation — he's not involved, he doesn't care, sometimes. Yes, that is a major departure from traditional Christian theology, but it has the distinct advantage of being faithful to the character and nature of the God revealed in Scripture. And it has other advantages as well.

For one thing, it explains quite well the world as we experience it — with all its beauty and horror. It accounts for why so many bad things happen: disease, famine, war, poverty, tsunamis, earthquakes, crime, corruption, and *Jersey*

Shore. The God who could allow (cause? ignore?) so much pain and suffering in our world strikes me as a lot like the God we encounter in certain passages of the Bible. In fancy terms, belief in a less-than-perfect God provides us with a theodicy: an explanation for evil. A paradoxical deity also explains why so many good things happen amidst the evil. God is a mixture of good and bad, and so is the world.

On a personal, and much more mundane, level maybe a paradoxical deity explains why I — created in the image of God — can at times feel deep frustration when dealing with my children, and in other moments, ineffable joy and love just looking at them. Or why I can at times be thoughtful and compassionate, and at others — many others — insensitive and rude. Maybe that is what it means to be created in the image of God: partly good and partly not.

Belief in a God who is capable of being cruel, vindictive, and misogynistic does not mean that we defend or condone those actions — just as Abraham did not support God's plan to destroy Sodom. We should not try to explain away or justify, for example, God's brutal treatment of his wife in Ezekiel or God's utterly pointless (as God admits) destruction of Job and his family. We should not ignore these texts or cook them up simply because God is not a paragon of virtue or a moral exemplar. Rather, we need to accept them as revelation of the character of God, without excusing God's actions. And we most certainly should never, ever point to God's immoral words and deeds as a justification for our own behavior.

We should, I propose, do more than not excuse God. We should hold God accountable. We should protest God's attitude and conduct. We should be bold enough to tell God what we think. Like a good teacher would welcome a student's challenge, God too is open to our assessments of his character, as he was with Abraham. Instead of offering God our praises, we should offer our appraisals. If you say God can do whatever God wants because he's God, I say: No way. I am not interested in being part of a religious tradition in which God can sanction the murder of tens of thousands of people and we don't bat an eye.

I am not only comfortable protesting God's actions — or inactions — in our world, but I also feel obligated to do so. I protest the pain and suffering, so much of it seemingly pointless and to those who least deserve it. How is it possible that God could create and preside over a world where little children die of hunger, where boys and girls are physically and sexually abused, where cruel dictators kill their own people? How could God stand by as six million Jews — his own chosen people! — are gassed to death? Yes, I get terribly exasperated that God seems to care so little. Where is God? Like Moses and Job and Jonah, I get angry and confused. Why doesn't God do something? I don't know why. But I do know that it fits with the God we find in the Bible. For every time God is lovingly or oppressively present in the biblical narrative, there are instances where God is conspicuously absent. Second Samuel, for example, is replete with stories right out of today's headlines: bloody civil war, rape, murder, incest, political corruption, and social injustice. God is not there either.

In light of such divine abandonment, it is very difficult for me to understand how some Christians believe that God has an interest and concern for the details of their life — if they should purchase a new house, take a new job, or paint the living room blue. How could God possibly care about those things when there are thousands of children around the world who at that very moment are suffering mightily? How can we presume that God cares so much about us, when he shows so little concern for so many others? Isn't that dreadfully naïve and self-centered of us? It seems to me that instead of petitioning God about our lives, maybe we should spend our time working alongside God — maybe even helping him, showing him the way, doing what he cannot or will not do — to make the world a better place.

Yes, God can be wonderfully loving, forgiving, and merciful. There are many moments where I experience the benevolent presence of God — in the beauty and majesty of nature, in quiet prayer and meditation, in time spent with family and loved ones. But God is not perfect, and I can live with that. Why must God be perfect? Why can't we love a God who is in the process of growing and developing? We show genuine love for flawed people all the time. To me, that is part of the powerful truth of the Incarnation: God became human, fully human — complex, imperfect, mutable — as a means of relating to us. Both we and God need to take responsibility for cultivating a living, mutual relationship by being willing to learn and change, work and argue. We must be open to love, which makes us vulnerable to hurt and anger and disappointment.

In short, for me, it makes sense that the dynamic, paradoxical God of the Bible is true revelation of the nature of the God of the universe. I suspect, however, that a number of Christians will be uncomfortable with — or strenuously object to — my proposed theology. That's fine. I don't like it either sometimes — I reserve the right to change my mind. I don't know where you stand — maybe you don't know either. That too is fine. These are sticky issues, and there are various approaches to digesting the unpalatable features of the biblical God. We do not each need to wrestle with God in the exact same way, but we do in fact need to strive and struggle; we must encounter the real God of the Bible for ourselves. Each of us, then, on our own and collectively, must read and study. We must converse with our pastors and teachers, consult commentaries, and talk with people from a variety of backgrounds and diverse perspectives. It will take some toil. There are no simple, easy resolutions; but that's okay. Life's not simple, the Bible's not easy, so why should we expect God to be? Let's have the courage and audacity to engage the raw and uncensored God of Scripture.

JESUS

If God is a complex and unsettling figure, we should expect the same to be true of the Son of God. And it is. Jesus is a chip off the ol' block. Our preachers give us a gentle Jesus, meek and mild, who loves you and all the little children of the world — red and yellow, black and white. That is the roasted rendition of the Gospels presented for our consumption. The real Jesus is too raw. The real Jesus does not say he loves you or the little children — actually, he says that to be his disciple, you must hate your own children (Luke 14:26).

"Hate children" is not a good answer to the question posed by the acronym WWJD: What would Jesus do? Nonetheless, it is a worthwhile question that we Christians can ask ourselves as we confront challenging life situations. But in order to speculate about what Jesus *would* do, we must first consider what Jesus *did* say and do. To do that, we must read the Gospels, all four of them, in their entirety. They aren't that long. We could easily read each one in less time than it takes to watch a movie — unless it's *The Lord of the Rings* trilogy. When we do, we just might be surprised by whom we meet.

Pastors, however, know that surprises lead to wrinkled brows and questions. So they play it safely and preach on carefully selected and isolated gospel texts, serving us a simple and palatable message. But when we work through the gospels from beginning to end, we discover strange and perplexing passages and unsavory images of the Savior. And we must be willing to make such discoveries. We must know the Jesus of Scripture. Not the Jesus of sermons and sound bites.

Most of our ideas about who Jesus is come from the Gospel of John. Here, Jesus preaches about himself, his mission and message, his relation to God, and about the need to believe in him for salvation. If you've got a red-letter Bible, note how the pages in John are bleeding. Jesus explains that he is the bread of life, the living water, the light of the world, the way, truth, and the life. He is God in the flesh. John's presentation of Jesus is inspiring and attractive. It is the one gospel most likely to move people to faith in Jesus. Hence, the famous John 3:16 — not Matthew, Mark, or Luke 3:16.

Obviously, John is a part of the Scripture, so it should certainly be taken into account as we formulate our understanding of Jesus. But it is only one of four. What about the first three gospels, the other 75 percent? The problem with them is that, well, they are problematic. Here Jesus, for example, asserts that his mission is only to the Jews, that his parables are intentionally confusing so that people will not repent and be saved, that one earns eternal life by keeping the Jewish law, that no one can be his disciple unless they sell all they have, that he came not to bring peace, but division, and that divorce and remarriage is adultery. Yes, it's raw stuff — which is why it is hardly ever served up in church. But if we digest only the diluted and domesticated Jesus we receive on Sunday, then there is no use for the Bible. We might as well decide who we want Jesus to be and go along our merry way. Or we can muster up some faith and fortitude to meet the real Jesus.

WHY WASN'T JESUS A CHRISTIAN?

Jesus was not a Christian. His name was not even Jesus.

He was a Jew. His name was Yeshua. He was born as a Jew to Jewish parents, named and circumcised as a Jew, lived as a Jew, followed Jewish laws, participated in Jewish rituals and festivals, and died as a Jew. This is a fact. Yes, he objected to the way in which the Jewish leaders of his day practiced their faith. But never does Jesus renounce Judaism and start a new religion. Rather, after Jesus died, his followers — who were also Jews — began the slow process of forming a new religious tradition separate from Judaism. Peter, Paul, James, Barnabas, Silas and others are essentially the founders of Christianity. Not Jesus.

The implications of Jesus' Jewishness are many. In general, to understand Jesus we really need to understand the Jewish tradition of Jesus' day and how it was situated in the larger Greco-Roman culture. But that takes a lot of effort, a lot of reading about weird sounding terms like "Greco-Roman." It is quite complex and difficult to address the fact that the man on whom our tradition is based was actually a member of a different religion. So it's one we aren't invited to think about very often.

Since Jesus was Jewish, it was natural for the first Christians to interpret the life of Jesus as the fulfillment and completion of the Jewish Scripture—that is, the Old Testament. Many Christians today assume—based on the preacher's poached version—that there are prophecies in the Old Testament which predict the coming of Jesus, that his birth, life, and crucifixion are foretold in the Old Testament and fulfilled in the New. This is not the case. It only takes a few minutes of looking back at the Old Testament to realize that there are no prophecies about Jesus, only passages which the gospel writers have applied to Jesus—and just how they have applied them may astonish you.

The very first time that the New Testament cites the Old Testament is a perfectly representative example. After Mary, the mother of Jesus, was found with child from the Holy Spirit (you can imagine Joseph's response to that), Matthew 1:22-23 says, "All this took place to fulfill what had been spoken by the Lord through the prophet: 'Look, a virgin shall conceive and bear a son, and they shall name him Immanuel,' which means 'God is with us.'" That looks straightforward enough, doesn't it? There must be a place in the Old Testament which predicts that the Messiah will be born of a virgin. But there isn't. Matthew is quoting Isaiah 7:14, as any study Bible indicates—this isn't highly classified information. So we need to look up Isaiah 7:14 and to comprehend Isaiah 7:14, we need to start reading at least at the beginning of Isaiah 7.

We might expect to find in Isaiah 7 something about a special woman, a miraculous birth, a future Messiah, a grand prediction—something that will connect to Jesus.

Instead we find ourselves in the middle of a confusing story about King Ahaz who is on the verge of being attacked by a coalition of armies. In response, God sends the prophet Isaiah to give him a message that everything will be well. In verses 10-17, God offers Ahaz a sign to accompany the message of hope. Verse 14 reads: "Therefore the Lord himself will give you a sign: Look, the young woman is with child and shall bear a son, and shall name him Immanuel." Verse 16 tells us the significance of the son: "Before the boy is able to reject the wrong and choose the right, the land of the two kings you dread will be laid waste." In other words, before the boy is very old — within the next few years — the threatening armies will be destroyed. (Incidentally, if you noticed that the Isaiah passage says "young woman," instead of "virgin," very good. We'll explain that in our final course, as it gets into different issues altogether.)

It's an unusual and mysterious oracle. But that's it. That's Isaiah 7:14 in its context — a story about a relatively obscure king, dealing with a minor military crisis, who gets a sign from God which involves an unnamed woman giving birth to an otherwise unknown son named Immanuel (not Jesus). Isaiah 7:14 is not a prophecy about a coming Messiah. It has nothing whatsoever to do with the birth of Jesus. Matthew, in short, has taken the verse out of its original context and applied it to Jesus.

It's the exact same scenario each of the numerous times that the gospel writers cite Old Testament texts. They take individual verses and apply them to Jesus in an effort to convince other Jews that Jesus was the Messiah. Feel free to check them out for yourself. Now this does not mean that the New Testament writers were lying or trying to trick you. It just means that the Old Testament does not predict Jesus any more than Nostradamus predicted Hitler (sorry, did not mean to put Jesus and Hitler in the same sentence). With enough creativity and imagination you can find in ancient texts "fulfilled predictions" for just about anything. Try it, it's kind of fun. Pick any chapter from Isaiah and show how a verse or two in it anticipates your own life in some way. It's easy to see, then, why the vast majority of Jews were not persuaded to become Christians.

WHAT IS THE KINGDOM OF GOD?

At the very heart of Jesus' message was his proclamation of the kingdom of God — or kingdom of heaven as it's called in Matthew. Jesus was always talking about it. The problem is that nobody really knows what he meant by "the kingdom." But that's not even the real problem. The real problem is that most Christians don't know that they don't know. Preachers never serve up the mystery of the kingdom for our consideration. It's quite remarkable both that the fundamental theme of Jesus' teaching is difficult to figure out, and that most of us aren't aware that there is something to figure out.

Here are a few samples of what Jesus says about the kingdom:

Since the time of John the Baptist, "the good news of the kingdom of God is preached, and every one enters it violently" (Luke 16:16). The kingdom "forcefully advances, and men of violence take it by force" (Matthew 11:12). It is not coming with signs to be observed, but rather "the kingdom of God is within you" (Luke 17:20-21). However, "if your eye causes you to sin, pluck it out; it is better for you to enter the kingdom of God with one eye than with two eyes to be thrown into hell" (Mark 9:47). In other places Jesus compares the kingdom to a farmer who sows seed, waits for the seed to grow, and then reaps the harvest (Mark 4:26-29); or to a grain of mustard seed that grows into a great tree, which, by the way, doesn't happen to mustard seeds (Luke 13:18-19); or to "yeast that a woman took and mixed in with three measures of flour until all of it was leavened" (Luke 13:20). Elsewhere Jesus associates the coming of the kingdom with his ability to cast out demons (Luke 14:20). Yes, the kingdom is a "mysterious secret" (Mark 4:10).

There are of course many other passages to consider, but the point is that it is very difficult to understand what the kingdom is—or where it is or when it is. The kingdom is taken by force by violent people? It's already here within us or among us? Entering it requires self-mutilation? And what do farmers, exorcisms, mustard seeds, and yeast have to do with it? These verses don't make for good poster board material; John 3:16 is much better for that. There's nothing simple and straightforward about Jesus; the very heart of his message is a "mystery" and a "secret," and he means for it to be that way. Imagine how easily Jesus could have explained what he meant by the kingdom of God. But he doesn't. Instead he gives us things to contemplate, opportunities to love God with our mind.

WHAT'S YOUR STORY?

Jesus liked to tell stories. Hard stories. Puzzling stories. We typically call them parables (not to be confused with two male cows). In church, however, parables are typically presented as stories with a clear message and meaning. They are neat little vignettes with a moral or theological point, a lesson for us to learn about some aspect of life or about

God. They are earthly stories with heavenly meanings, we are told. But the unprocessed, unfiltered parables are a bit more complicated than that. Jesus himself says so. As a rule of thumb, it's always a good idea to see if Jesus has anything to say about a subject—that's a good place to start. In this case, Jesus explains that he teaches with parables precisely so that the kingdom of God will remain a secret.

In Mark 4:10-12, Jesus says to his disciples: "To you [the disciples] has been given the secret of the kingdom of God, but for those outside, everything comes in parables, in order that they may look, but not perceive, and may listen, but not understand, lest they turn and be forgiven." Why would Jesus tell the secret or mystery of the kingdom only to the disciples? What about everybody else, all those people who need to be reached with the good news? Not to mention us—the millions of Christian readers through the centuries—who are also left wondering about the secret of the kingdom. Remarkably, Jesus says that he uses parables precisely so that people will be confused and *not* understand, otherwise they might repent and be forgiven. Rather than trying desperately to help people learn, to save their souls, Jesus purposefully obscures the truth so that they won't believe. Huh? Furthermore, according to Mark 4:34, Jesus only taught by parables and only explained things in private to his disciples. What about the masses—plus the people at the Masses—who need to hear the Gospel message?

Based on Jesus' own explicit statements, then, we should not expect the parables to be easy reads. When we stop to think about them and probe them a bit, we realize this fairly quickly. Parables are not cool stories with a moral lesson; they are not like Aesop's fables. Rather, parables are meant to make us think; they stir curiosity and imagination.

They invite us into the narrative and prompt us to engage it; they are stories with twists, unexpected conclusions. They set us up for one thing and then pull the rug out from under us — and who hasn't had that happen to them.

Jesus seemingly wanted his audience to cogitate — to think and rethink. He did not give them answers; he did not even give them matching, multiple choice, or true-false questions (which, seriously, is one of the reasons that I don't give them to my students either — they are just plain ungodly). Rather he opened a space for conversation by telling a story. Jesus required active, participatory learning. Such a pedagogical style makes more demands on the reader. It requires hard work. We aren't handed a simple point. Instead, we are given a riddle that we must solve — and even then there isn't only one solution. By using parables, perhaps Jesus is teaching us that learning to live with open ends, with ambiguity, is part of developing a mature, grown-up faith. Jesus isn't the answer; Jesus is the question.

There's quite a nice, big point to be made here. Do you see it? . . . Jesus' own teaching style mirrors the nature of the whole Bible. The Bible itself functions much like a parable. Doesn't this make perfect sense: Jesus does not give us easy stories, and God does not give us an easy Book. The Word of God always requires arduous work.

Let's start with a popular, palatable parable often proffered by our preachers. The parable of the Prodigal Son in Luke 15 is a simple one: it's a story about God's amazing love for us — no matter what we do, God will always take us back — and how we should show the same kind of love and forgiveness to others. But is that the extent of what's going on here? Can the parable be boiled down to that one idea? On second glance, seemingly not. If that's the message

Jesus intended, he certainly could've told a more straight-forward story. A close reading of this passage raises a number of interesting questions which complicate matters. For example:

Common sense dictates that we don't give our children their inheritance when they are young, so why does the father do this? What kind of father has this man been to have raised such an irresponsible child who clearly has some issues (think Lindsay Lohan)? Don't we tend to hold the parents at least partially responsible for a kid who turns out so badly? But then again, wouldn't most fathers welcome their son back home? Is there anything unusual or unique about that kind of love? Is the prodigal truly remorseful? Or does he just want a second chance? Does he suffer any consequences for his actions? If not, is that the message we want to send to our children: live licentiously and the slate will be wiped clean? If the theological point is about how God loves us or the moral point is how we are to show mercy and forgiveness toward others, then why include the part about the older brother? That makes things messier, especially since most people identify with the older sibling. Why does he feel that his loyalty has not been adequately acknowledged? Does this again reflect poorly on the father? Don't we feel sympathy for the older son? Herein lies the unexpected twist: the party is for the prodigal, not the good son. It's for the guy who partied with the prostitutes, not the one who graduated with a 4.0. This is the prickly part of the story. It is the part that is unnecessary if Jesus is trying to teach about love and compassion. We are never told if the older son goes to the party or not. We are left hanging, wondering about his final response, which distracts our focus from the father's benevolent treatment of the younger son.

Imagine how easily Jesus could have told a clear-cut story about forgiveness. We could come up with one in five minutes—it could even involve Lindsay. But Jesus doesn't give us that. He makes it more strenuous.

WHAT IS THAT SUPPOSED TO MEAN?

If familiar parables like the Prodigal Son are not nearly as elementary as we might have been led to believe, imagine how much stranger others might be. Two such parables surround the story of the Prodigal, namely, that of the Great Dinner and the Dishonest Manager (different Bibles give them different titles). You won't find these on your plate very often.

Luke 14:15-24 is about a man hosting a fancy dinner, but his RSVPs came back negative. So the man instructs his servant to go out into the streets and bring in the poor, crippled, lame, and blind. When that is done, there is still room, so the man again instructs the servant to find people and compel them to come to the banquet. It ends with the man saying, "For I tell you, none of those who were invited will taste my dinner."

Questions abound. Why is the man so upset with the invited guests who cannot come? They have reasonably good excuses—one must deal with a recent real estate purchase and one has gotten married—and they all politely decline, saying, "Please accept my regrets." Why is the man so insistent that the banquet be well attended? Does he genuinely care about the poor, lame, and blind? Or does he just not want to be embarrassed by having no one show up to his party? If he were really concerned about the disenfranchised, why not invite them first? If we read it allegorically, is the banquet the kingdom of God and who do the invited people represent — the Jews? But then why does it say "none" of those invited will taste the dinner — aren't there Jews who are part of the kingdom? Alternatively, maybe they represent people too concerned with the affairs of this world to partake in the dinner party/kingdom (uh oh, getting married and buying houses — that could be me)? And who do the poor, lame, and blind represent? Hopefully not the poor, lame, and blind, because very few of us fall into those categories.

The parable of the Dishonest Manager in Luke 16:1-9 is another tough one — although perhaps not as cool, as we go from wild parties to CPA offices, from Lindsay Lohan to Bernie Madoff. Here, a rich man had a manager — an accountant or finance officer — who was losing money for him, or perhaps stealing it. When the rich man discovers this, he fires the manager, who then devises a plan to save himself from the problems of losing his job. He approaches the people who owe his master money and reduces their bill. The rich man, in turn (verse 8), "commended the dishonest manager because he had acted shrewdly; for the children of this age are more shrewd in dealing with their own generation than the children of light."

That's a brow-wrinkler. What is meant by the "children of this age" and the "children of light" — it sounds as if it's better to be the former than the latter, which is odd? Why praise the manager for doing "creative accounting" in order to save himself? In verse nine it gets even more perplexing: "I tell you, make friends for yourselves by means of dishonest wealth, so that when it is gone, they may welcome you into their eternal homes." What is "dishonest wealth" — is this an allusion to Wall Street? Furthermore, what are eternal homes? Surely it can't be heaven, because then you get in by being a cheat. And is he suggesting that we employ ill-gotten gain to make beneficial social connections? What in the world does Jesus mean by this parable?

HOW CAN I BE A SHEEP?

Sometimes Jesus' stories are difficult because their meaning is unclear. In other cases, the meaning is easier to discern, but the resulting "message" is difficult.

The parable in Matthew 25:31-46 explains who will enter the kingdom and who will be banished into eternal torment. That's crucial information. This is as big as it gets. We must pay attention so we can be part of the kingdom. But, alas, we aren't fed this one very often because it makes most of us uncomfortable.

In the story, the Son of Man sits on his throne and judges the peoples of the earth, separating them into two groups, the sheep and the goats. The sheep are those who feed the hungry, give drink to the thirsty, welcome strangers, clothe the naked, take care of the sick, and visit those in prison (where you might see Lindsay and Bernie). The goats are the people who don't do these acts of charity. What does the Son of Man say to the sheep? "Come, you who are blessed by my Father, inherit the kingdom." And what about the goats? "Depart from me into the eternal fire prepared for the devil and his angels."

Jesus spells out quite clearly how to enter the kingdom: Take care of the less fortunate. One's ticket to the kingdom is earned by benevolent actions, not making a confessional statement. There really isn't much to interpret here. If we don't spend our lives feeding the hungry, clothing the naked, and caring for the poor, where does that leave us? When this text is addressed, it is undoubtedly part of a "social gospel" message meant to inspire us to live more charitably. Such sermons, however, routinely gloss over the fact that those who fail to love the oppressed are condemned to eternal punishment along with the devil. That's the raw part that makes us uncomfortable. The goats are probably uncomfortable, too, in that "eternal fire."

A second fairly transparent parable is the Rich Fool (Luke 12:13-21). Jesus even tells us up front what this one is about: It serves as a warning "against all kinds of greed; for one's life does not consist in the abundance of possessions." The story concerns a wealthy man whose barns were not big enough to store all of his crops. So he tore them down and built bigger barns. He then says to himself, "I have ample goods laid up for many years. I will relax, eat, drink, and be merry" to which God responds, "You fool! Tonight your life is demanded of you. And the things you have prepared, whose will they be?"

This one is no role in the hay (in the barn, get it?). Its' difficult—more like trying to find a needle in the haystack (though I am not sure who does that, maybe people who get rugs pulled out from under them). Preachers chocolate-frost this one with interpretations like, "This is merely a warning about putting money before God. Just keep God first and you'll be fine." But is that right? If ever there were a passage that spoke directly to our idea of saving and investing for retirement, this is it. Think about how diligently preachers work to make other Bible passages meaningful for our contemporary world, and here is one that requires no effort— it drips with relevancy. The man is simply accumulating wealth so that he will be comfortable in the future. He is not

Jesus

being dishonest or wicked. It does not say that he hoarded his wealth and gave away none of it. He is merely planning for tomorrow by building a larger retirement portfolio. For Jesus, that *is* being greedy.

Build bigger barns at your own risk. Or perhaps, follow Jesus' teaching at your own risk.

CUT OFF MY WHAT?

Jesus did not always tell stories. Sometimes he preached. When Jesus preaches, we should listen.

Jesus' most famous sermon is the Sermon on the Mount found in Matthew 5-7. It begins with the well-known Beatitudes—blessed are the pure in heart, the meek, and so on. Not as well-known is the fact that there are two separate versions of the Beatitudes; the other is in Luke 6:20-23, which is part of the Sermon on the Plain. Here are a couple of selections from each gospel:

Matthew's version: Blessed are the poor in spirit, for theirs is the kingdom of heaven. Blessed are those who hunger and thirst for righteousness, for they will be filled.

Luke's version: Blessed are you who are poor, for yours is the kingdom of God. Blessed are you who are hungry now, for you will be filled.

Preachers typically give us the ones from Matthew for obvious reasons. It's much easier to be poor *in spirit* and to hunger *for righteousness*—those are spiritual ideas. Anyone can do that. Luke's version, by contrast, is physical, literal: Blessed are those who are poor and hungry. Who wants to be those things? Most of us are not poor—certainly not by global standards (if you have a TV, you are not poor); and for goodness sakes, we are not hungry—missing lunch does

99

not count. Luke's version doesn't come off too well in the mouth of a portly preacher in a dapper suit.

There's another reason to ignore Luke's text. Following the Beatitudes are the less popular "Woes" — a strong term of warning with highly negative connotations. It's not hard to see why they don't preach very well: "Woe to you who are rich, for you have received your consolation. Woe to you who are full now, for you will be hungry. Woe to you who are laughing now, for you will mourn and weep." Notice that Jesus does not say, "Woe to the rich who hoard their money, or who don't share their wealth, or who don't give food to the poor." No, it's just woe to the rich. Period. Again, it's hard not to point out that "rich, full, and laughing" is a fairly good description of many preachers: financially comfortable, well-fed, and smiling.

Jesus' Sermon only gets better — or worse. In Matthew 5:17-20 Jesus claims that he has come not to abolish the Jewish law and the prophets but to fulfill them. He then asserts that "whoever breaks [or annuls] one of the least of the commandments, and teaches others to do the same, will be called least in the kingdom of heaven." Here Jesus teaches that we should keep the Jewish law, that is, all the regulations in the Old Testament. Similarly, in Luke 16:17 he says, "It is easier for heaven and earth to pass away than for one stroke of a letter of the law to be dropped." How much clearer could Jesus be? If we want to follow what he teaches, then we must obey the Jewish laws — all 613 of them, including those deeply troubling ones that we sampled earlier. In fact, in Mark 7:9-10 Jesus criticizes the Jewish leaders for not adhering to the laws and he names one that ought to be followed: "Whoever speaks evil of father or mother must surely die" (okay, it's not that bad of a law if you've got a teenager). It may be disconcerting, but Jesus' insistence on the permanent validity of the law makes quite a bit of sense, since, after all, Jesus is the Incarnation of the lawgiver.

But Christians don't keep the Jewish laws. Why? Because Paul says we don't have to. Indeed, Jesus' statement is directly contrary to what Paul teaches in a number of places, for example, in Romans 10:4 where he says that "Christ is the end of the law so that there may be righteousness for everyone who believes." (Paul knew it would be difficult to obtain male Gentile converts if circumcision were required, especially with no anesthesia.) Christianity has opted to follow Paul, the much easier route. Jesus' words are simply disregarded. More on this later.

Actually, according to Jesus, one has to do more than follow the laws: "Unless your righteousness exceeds that of the scribes and the Pharisees, you will never enter the kingdom of heaven" (Matthew 5:20). Jesus then gives us six examples of how our righteousness must surpass that of the law-abiding scribes and Pharisees. We should pay close attention if we plan to enter the kingdom. First, he cites the standards of the scribes and Pharisees, with the phrase, "You have heard it said . . ." And then indicates how one goes beyond it with the phrase, "But I say to you . . ." Take a moment to read this passage carefully for yourself (Matthew 5:21-48), keeping in mind that if we don't live up to these standards, we will "never enter the kingdom of heaven." Here is what Jesus says followed by a few of my thoughts and questions, which unfortunately, though not surprisingly, he does not answer.

Jesus: You have heard it said, "Don't murder and anyone who does will be subject to judgment." But I say to you that anyone who gets angry with another person will be subject to judgment and anyone who says "You fool!" is in danger of the fires of hell.

Me: Well, darn, the very first one and I am out of the kingdom. How can we never get angry? Isn't anger a natural and inevitable human emotion? Surely it's better to get angry with someone than to murder them? And I thought it was another F-word that would get me in trouble.

Jesus: You have heard that it was said, "You shall not commit adultery." But I say to you that anyone who looks at a woman lustfully has already committed adultery with her in his heart. If your right eye causes you to stumble, gouge it out. If your right hand causes you to sin, cut it off. For it's better to lose one body part than to have your whole body thrown into hell.

Me: Now I am definitely out on this one, way out. Is it possible never to have an impure thought about another woman? I am only human. God made me that way. Are you being serious about poking out your eye and cutting off your hand? Is that some veiled reference to auto-erotic behavior? Oh, and what about women lusting after men? I can't look at another woman but my wife can drool (sometimes literally) over Brad Pitt and George Clooney?

Jesus: You have heard it said, "Anyone who divorces his wife must give her a certificate of divorce." But I say to you that whoever divorces his wife, except for infidelity, and marries another commits adultery against her; and if she divorces her husband and marries another, she commits adultery. And whoever marries a divorced woman commits adultery.

Me: Well, then I know a lot of people who are living in adulterous marriages. In fact, the church is full of them. You must really be against divorce since you give this command three more times in the gospels (Matthew 19:9; Mark 10:11-12; Luke 16:18 — the quote from Jesus here is actually a combination of the four passages), and on two of them, you don't even both to mention the phrase "except for infidelity." Why is that? What's more is that Paul affirms your view in 1 Corinthians 7:10-11, which is striking since Paul rarely refers to your teachings.

Boy, this is a trying word, probably no less radical in your day than it is now. I am thinking the same thing that your disciples said (Matthew 19:8-11): It's best not to get married. You told them that they were right. But then what you said next freaks me out. I mean really gives me the heebie jeebies, Jesus. You said, "For there are eunuchs who were born that way, and there are eunuchs who have been made eunuchs by others, and there are those who have made themselves eunuchs for the sake of the kingdom of heaven. The one who can accept this should accept it." A eunuch is an emasculated male, a guy without testicles. Jesus, what in the world do you mean? At best, you appear to be advocating a life of celibacy over marriage; at worst, you are commending self-emasculation, cutting off my manhood! That's a painful thought. Surely you jest. No? Then I will have to think twice about what you stated earlier concerning gouging out my eye and cutting off my hand. I couldn't imagine that you were speaking literally, but maybe you were.

Alright, let's forget this stuff about cutting off body parts. I get your point: Divorce and remarriage is adultery. There really is no way around the plain meaning of what you say. Imagine how empty churches would be if pastors condemned second marriages — and third and fourth and fifth.

Jesus: You have heard that it was said, "Do not break your oath, but fulfill to the Lord the vows you have made." But I say to you that there is no need to swear an oath under any circumstance. You need only say, "Yes" or "No."

Me: Alright I can do this. That's one.

Jesus: You have heard it said, "Eye for eye, and tooth for tooth." But I say that you must not resist an evil person. If anyone slaps you on the right cheek, turn to them the other cheek as well. And if anyone wants to sue you and take your shirt, hand over your coat as well. Give to the one who asks you, and do not turn away from the one who wants to borrow from you.

Me: Back to the toughies, I see. So we must be pacifists — no joining the military? We can never try to stop someone who is doing evil? And we cannot ever act in self-defense? And if someone sues us for one thousand dollars we are supposed to pay them two thousand? Do you mean we should give money to every charity that solicits us, every homeless person on the street corner? I did try to turn the other cheek when my mama whipped on the behind, but I don't know if that counts.

Jesus: You have heard it said, "You shall love your neighbor and hate your enemy." But I say that you should love your enemies, bless those who curse you, do good to those who hate you, and pray for those who persecute you. Therefore you are to be perfect, just as your Father in heaven is perfect.

Me: Well, I guess that makes sense. If you cannot resist an evil doer, you might as well try to love them, hard as that is. But what's this about being perfect just like God is? Preachers frequently remind us that we don't have to be perfect. But yet you command us in no uncertain terms: Be perfect.

THE PRINCE OF PEACE? OR PIECE?

Among the other enigmatic and unsettling teachings of Jesus scattered throughout the Gospels is Matthew 10:34, where Jesus claims, "Do not think that I have come to bring peace to the earth; I have not come to bring peace, but a sword." Similarly in Luke 12:50—following another vexing statement about bringing fire to the earth—Jesus asks rhetorically, "Do you think I have come to bring peace to the earth? No, I tell you, but rather division." Based on these words Jesus is not the Prince of Peace, but the Prince of Piece. In both Matthew and Luke, Jesus then specifies the nature of the violence and division that he intends to bring, namely, to set sons against fathers, daughters against mothers, and in-laws against each other (as if we need Jesus to help us with that). Furthermore, whoever loves their parents or their children more than Jesus is not worthy to be his disciple. In Luke 14:26 it's even harsher: "Whoever comes to me and does not hate father and mother, wife and children, brothers and sisters, yes, even life itself, cannot be my disciple."

Pastors typically baste this one by saying: "Sometimes families are divided over Jesus. If one family member is a Christian and the other is not, there will be strife and conflict. And as for not loving, or even hating your family members, Jesus is just making the point that following him requires complete and total commitment. It's about the cost of discipleship—we have to be prepared to give up our lives. He doesn't literally mean for you to hate your life and family." Okay. But it would be nice if that is what Jesus actually said. Instead, Jesus insists that his purpose is to turn family members against each other; it's not simply a result of his ministry. He came expressly in order to bring violence and division—that's his goal. If you don't hate life itself you cannot be a follower of Jesus. Even if we go with the pastor's spin on it, how many Christians totally "give up" (instead of "hate") their lives to follow Jesus? What percentage of your sixteen waking hours each day is spent in direct service to God? Women, by the way, should note that hating your husband is not on the list; men should note that if you hate your wife, hating your life won't be a problem.

Of course, it would be preferable if Jesus didn't say these things; then we wouldn't have to try to explain them away. What would we Christians say about Islam if Mohammed had made these statements in the Koran?

THE END IS NIGH, BUT HOW NIGH?

Jesus frequently taught in parables. He sometimes sermonized. And he occasionally sounded like a crazy man who thought the world was coming to an end very soon. But it wasn't—obviously. For example, in Mark 13, Jesus proclaims: "But in those days, following that distress, the sun will be darkened, and the moon will not give its light; the stars will fall from the sky, and the heavenly bodies will be shaken. Then people will see the Son of Man coming on the clouds with great power and glory. He will send out the angels, and gather his elect from the four winds, from the ends of the earth to the ends of the heaven" (13:24-27).

I know, I know, how in the world does Jesus think that the moon gives off light. Doesn't he know it only reflects sunlight? Oh, and then there is the other minor issue: the Son of Man coming on the clouds. This certainly sounds like the second coming of Christ, the so-called "rapture." When will this happen? Jesus tells us a few verses later: "Truly I tell you, this generation will not pass away until all these things have taken place." What? Why would Jesus say this? There are no cataclysmic events in the heavens, followed by the Son of Man appearing on the clouds during the disciples' lifetime. Doesn't happen.

It is clear that many of Jesus' earliest followers, including Paul, thought that Jesus would return before they died, that is, during "this generation" just as Jesus said. This strand of Jesus' teaching is a potential source of embarrassment for Christianity. It appears as though Jesus was wrong. Let's mull this over for a second: If Jesus knew that the church would be here two thousand years later, couldn't he have easily spelled that out: "I am going to die, and be raised from the dead, which will serve to save human kind from their sins. Then at some point in the far distant future, too far to say really, I will return and bring the world to an end." But no. Instead, he says to his own followers that the Son of Man will arrive on the clouds during their generation.

"WHAT MUST I DO TO INHERIT ETERNAL LIFE?"

We've sampled texts in which Jesus teaches in parables or sermons about how to enter the kingdom — whatever exactly the kingdom is. But what about his conversations with people and, more crucially, what about "eternal life"?

Happily, Mark 10:17-31 and Luke 18:18-25 feature a scene in which a man directly asks Jesus, "Good Teacher, what must I do to inherit eternal life?" Alright, here it comes: the answer to the six million dollar question (or maybe nowadays, the six billion dollar question—by the time this manuscript goes to press, six trillion).

Before answering the question, Jesus asks a question of his own, "Why do you call me good? No one is good but God alone." Oh, dear, before we can even get to the answer, Jesus is saying more bizarre stuff. Is he denying his divinity? If Jesus is God, why would he make such misleading statements—wouldn't this have been a wonderful opportunity for him to affirm his divine status?

Alright, alright here's the answer we've been waiting for. Jesus tells the man that he inherits eternal life by . . . drum roll . . . keeping the Ten Commandments. Gong. When the man replies that he has obeyed the laws, Jesus declares, "There is still one thing you lack. Sell all that you own and give the money to the poor; and you will have treasure in heaven; then come follow me" (Luke 18:22). The man is saddened, for he apparently is unwilling to part with his wealth. Jesus then adds, "How hard it is for those who have wealth to enter the kingdom of God. In fact, it is easier for a camel to go through the eye of a needle than for someone who is rich to enter the kingdom of God."

There's the real, raw Jesus. You obtain eternal life by keeping the Jewish laws—or at least the Ten Commandments—and giving up all your possessions. Couldn't be any clearer—unless he had carved it into Mount Rushmore, say, right across George Washington's forehead. We may be puzzled by Jesus' answer, but surely we should take it seriously. What Jesus himself says about eternal life is kind of important. At least his answer here is consistent with the Sermon on the Mount: you must keep the law and then some.

Preachers might sauté this passage by asserting that Jesus is talking only to this one man, not you and me. True enough. But none of the gospels are addressed specifically to us, so in that case nothing Jesus says has any relevance for any of us today. Maybe we could conclude that since Jesus has not yet died, the best way to God is through following Jewish law. That doesn't really work though. If Jesus knew that belief in his death and resurrection was the way to eternal life, then why wouldn't he simply have said so?

Another typical response is that Jesus is using hyperbole — he doesn't literally mean to give up everything you own. He is merely making the point that we shouldn't put material possessions before God. Similar explanations are offered for other difficult anti-wealth sayings of Jesus, like the one in Luke 14:33: "No one can become my disciple if you do not give up all your possessions." In church you are sure to hear things such as, "Wealth in itself is not bad. It's the love of money — not money itself — that is wrong. Just keep your priorities in order." Talk about misquoting Jesus. According to Jesus, wealth is bad. Pure and simple. It prevents you from inheriting eternal life and it keeps you out of the kingdom — a camel cannot go through the eye of a needle.

Consider this: Imagine if Jesus had said that it's easier for a camel to go through the eye of a needle than for a murderer to enter the kingdom of God. Would preachers then say, "Murder in itself is not bad, it's the love of murdering that is wrong — it's when you put murdering before God that it becomes bad"? Of course not. That's ridiculous, because we think of murdering as so obviously wrong. Apparently Jesus thought the same thing about wealth.

DID JESUS CURSE? AND WAS HE RACIST?

This section is PG-13 for adult language.

Jesus wasn't always Mr. Nice Guy. He did not always practice what he preached. He taught that we are to love our enemies and pray for those who persecute us (Matthew 5:39, 44). Yet he himself repeatedly hurls insults at those who oppose him. He calls the Pharisees an evil "brood of vipers," that is, "children of snakes," which, at best, is tantamount to calling them SOBs. Actually, according to most commentators, it's worse; "brood of vipers" is an offensive term of contempt meaning, "sons of the devil" (Matthew 12:34). That's exactly what Jesus said in John 8 to a group of antagonists: "Why do you not hear what I am saying? It is because you cannot understand my word. You are of your father, the devil." To put it in contemporary terms, Jesus says: "Do you understand the words that are coming out of my mouth? No! Now just go to hell where you belong."

On two separate occasions the Jewish leaders ask Jesus for a sign—a seemingly reasonable request which Jesus could have granted in an effort to win them over. Instead, he refuses, calling them "wicked and adulterous" (Matthew 12:38-45; 16:1-4). Jesus slanders their morality and sexuality. We too have curses which insult a person's sexuality; we (I mean, I don't, but people do) call them "fornicators," which of course is the F-word. Yes, let's be frank, Jesus basically calls them "wicked f … kers." Jesus also uses the other F-word. In one of his tirades against the Pharisees, he calls them "blind fools" (Matthew 23:17). Jesus, you recall, had warned that anyone who says "You fool" is in danger of the fire of hell. We might also ask how overturning the tables of the moneychangers in the temple adheres to Jesus' own command to "turn the other cheek" and "not resist an evildoer."

Yes, these are instances of Jesus lashing out at his enemies. But isn't that the point. Jesus himself taught to "love your enemies" and he asked rhetorically, "If you love those who love you, what reward will you get? Don't even the tax collectors do that?"

Jesus could be caustic not only to his adversaries, but also to his friends. There are several scenes when he comes off as rude, harsh, and insensitive to potential followers, his own family, and those who seek healing. For example, in Luke 9:57-62 (see also Matthew 18:18-22), several different people express a desire to participate in Jesus' ministry. The first person says to Jesus, "I will follow you wherever you go," to which Jesus replies, "Foxes have holes, and birds of the air have nests, but the Son of Man has nowhere to lay his head." The second person says, "Lord, let me first go and bury my father," to which Jesus says, "Let the dead bury their own dead." Similarly, the third declares, "I will follow you, Lord; but first let me say goodbye to those at my home," to which Jesus says, "No one who puts a hand to the plow and looks back is fit for the kingdom of God."

Jesus' retorts, presumably, are meant to convey the difficult nature of being a disciple, the total commitment required. But, still, here are people who sincerely wish to follow Jesus, yet he is terse and unwelcoming. He could have made the same point in a more sensitive manner: "I recognize that your father's funeral is tomorrow or that you'd like to say farewell to your family, but being a disciple will demand great sacrifice, so you might as well start now." Instead, his acidulous replies are unappealing. He is hardly a warm and loving Jesus who is desirous "that all should be saved."

In another passage someone tells Jesus that his mother and brothers are standing outside wanting to speak with him, to which Jesus says, "Who is my mother, and who are my brothers?" Then looking around at his disciples he remarks, "Here are my mother and my brothers. For whoever does the will of God is my brother and sister and mother" (Mark 3:31-35 and Matthew 12:46–50). Again, we get Jesus' point. But does he need to be so dismissive to his own family, especially his mother. I would like to have seen the look on Mary's face.

The Pharisees, his family, his friends — maybe we could forgive Jesus for moments of anger and callousness with them. But a poor Canaanite woman seeking healing for her little girl?

In Matthew 15:21-28 (see also Mark 7:24-30) a woman cries out to Jesus asking him to deliver her daughter from demonic possession. Initially, he ignored her. But her persistent shouting was annoying the disciples, so they ask Jesus to send her away. He then explains why he will not acknowledge her: "I was sent only to the lost sheep of Israel." The woman is not an Israelite (a Jew); nonetheless she is not to be denied. She approaches Jesus, kneels at his feet, and pleads, "Lord, help me!" Still, Jesus refuses, "It is not right to take the children's bread and throw it to the dogs." Ouch! Jesus calls this Canaanite woman — a suffering mother of an ill child who has sought mercy and healing from him — a "dog" because of her ethnicity. Is Jesus being racist? Let's be honest, he is more-or-less calling her a Gentile B who isn't worthy of his time. Remarkably, however, the woman argues with Jesus by offering a witty comeback (You go, girl): "Yes, Lord, but even the dogs eat the crumbs that fall from the master's table." Jesus then changes his mind and decides to grant her request—only, however, after she accepts her status as a dog.

Jesus' incredibly harsh treatment of this beleaguered woman is unpalatable to say the least. But why would Jesus say that he was sent only to the "lost sheep of the house of Israel"—that his mission was to Jews exclusively, not Gentiles. This is a particularly odd statement for Jesus to make if he thought of himself as we think of him—the savior of everyone. How could Jesus himself have known that he was going to suffer and die for the sins of the world, and yet treat this woman so rudely simply because she wasn't Jewish?

RAW REFLECTIONS

So WWRRJD—what would the real raw Jesus do? As Christians attempting to answer that question, we must take the Gospels—all four of them—as serious, meaningful revelation about the nature and character of Jesus and his message. As with our study of God in the previous course, we cannot cop out and say that we won't ever understand these difficult passages which preachers rarely serve us. We do comprehend them. They are just hard to swallow. Yes, there are other more appetizing images of Jesus. But what about the tough ones? How are we to digest them? Again, I offer two reflections, the first indispensable, the second dispensable.

First, just as we must love God by wrestling with God, so we must also live out our faith by wrestling with God in the flesh, Jesus. Paralleling the host of Old Testament characters who struggled with God are people in the Gospels, like the Canaanite woman, who argue with Jesus. The disciples bicker with Jesus about who will sit at his right hand. Peter questions Jesus about most everything. Mary confronts Jesus about her sister Martha's failure to help her. These characters undoubtedly have deep relationships with Jesus, not in spite of, but because of their willingness to challenge and engage him. They grow as a result. And so does Jesus, it seems, who relates to them in a genuinely open-ended fashion. Reminiscent of God who, at Abraham's prodding, reconsiders his plan to destroy everyone in Sodom, Jesus too changes his mind about the appropriateness of helping a Gentile woman as a result of his encounter with one.

That's part of the powerful truth of the incarnation. God became human — a human who lived in a real time and place, faced real problems, interacted openly with real people, and experienced real internal struggles. Isn't that what it means to say that Jesus was fully human? If God relates to us, with us, through the human Jesus, we then must relate to God with our humanity. Naturally, then, Jesus offers us opportunities to employ our most uniquely of human capacities: our mind, our ability to reason.

The raw Jesus invites — requires — us to think, to love God with our brains. In the unfiltered Gospels, we find a Jesus who does not give answers. He typically responds to questions with an enigmatic parable, a puzzling retort, or by asking a question in return. Jesus is not big on answers, at least not transparent ones. Rather, he seems to be interested in prompting us to engage. Jesus gives us fresh food for thought. Perhaps Jesus would respond to WWJD by asking

WWYD—what would you do?—thereby opening space for cogitation and conversation.

The first three courses of our meal, then, are beginning to develop some common elements, a theme is emerging: The diversity of the Bible presents us with a variety of views and perspectives, sometimes inconsistent ones, which calls us to enter the dialogue. God is a complex, mysterious, at times deeply troubling figure with whom we must strive and contend. And now the incarnation of God in the person of Jesus necessitates our active participation with his edgy, provocative sayings and complex interactions with others.

While it may be tricky to know what Jesus would do, wouldn't it be fair to say that he would want us to be mature, responsible people of faith who are bold enough to deal with these hard-to-stomach passages? Wouldn't he want us to address them openly and honestly, not seeking quick, easy, and diluted explanations that begin with "What Jesus was really trying to say was . . ." or "He did not literally mean . . ." Preachers resort to such statements when they know that taking Jesus at his word is going to be problematic. Yes, there is a place for symbolic or allegorical readings. But in cases where we are served up an interpretation which is at odds with the plain sense of the text, it is likely a deep fried Gospel. If in doubt, we must take the raw version and assume that Jesus meant what he said.

If we flay away what we do not like about Jesus and the Gospels, and accept only what we find palatable, then we are the ones who are forming Jesus in our own image—rather than being transformed by Jesus. When we start playing Create-a-Jesus, Scripture becomes pointless—we might as well rewrite the whole thing to say exactly what we want—and Jesus becomes nothing more than a projection of our own beliefs and principles.

We as Christians have a tendency to see Jesus as a reflection of ourselves—ethnically, spiritually, socially and culturally, and morally and ethically. In African Christianity, Jesus is imagined as dark skinned, in white churches he's white, in Asian communities he's Asian, and so on. Jesus doesn't love the red and yellow, black and white children of the world. He becomes red and yellow, black and white. In a middle-class, suburban church we are likely to be presented with a white-collar Jesus who has excellent executive leadership skills. If our audience is a group of teenage girls, we might suggest that Jesus is your boyfriend (not sure how it goes if your audience is male). If we are in a poor, rural setting—or a "liberal" church—we will be served stories about Jesus' concern for the impoverished and disenfranchised. If we need a message about high moral standards, we preach on Jesus' ability to resist temptation in the wilderness. If we are looking for a redneck Jesus, we can find that too—after all, he was a carpenter who loved fishing. And the list goes on. The Gospels, in short, are a mirror rather than a window.

It is no wonder then that so many people are comfortable with Jesus. Gentle Jesus, meek and mild, is our friend. He is the manifestation of our hopes and dreams, of who we are. He is indistinguishable from our ethnic, cultural, and religious norms and values. But forcing someone to conform to our own image is not respecting or loving them, and that includes Jesus.

Now, let's be clear. Everyone reads the Bible from a certain location with certain predispositions. Everyone comes from somewhere. I do too. I am not claiming to promote an objective view of Jesus, as if I can escape my own context.

What I am asserting is that we need to be aware of the ways in which cultural, social, and religious location influence the way in which we see and relate to Jesus. We need to understand that people create Jesus in their own image. This is an essential first step in meeting the raw Jesus of the Gospels. The second step is to try to allow Jesus to be revealed to us. We must exercise that uniquely human ability to step outside ourselves and — even if we cannot do it perfectly — let Jesus be separate from us, Other, different. Not a reflection of ourselves. And we do that by undertaking a truthful, thorough, and unbiased study of Scripture. For starters, you might try reading through one of the gospels and substituting the name Yeshua for Jesus.

At night when you are inside, a window can function as a mirror if you are too far away from it. You simply see your own reflection. But when you get up close to the glass, with your face right against it, it becomes a window again and you can see through it to the world outside. That's what we must do with the gospels: get right up on it — studying diligently and analyzing carefully — so that it functions as it's supposed to, as a window to the truth outside of ourselves, not a mirror reflection of ourselves.

The Jewish religious leaders, at least according to the gospel narratives, hated Jesus so much that they wanted to kill him. Why? Because he challenged their authority. He criticized them for "abandoning the commandments of God and holding instead to human tradition," for rejecting the truth of the Word of God in favor of their own biased and bogus interpretations of it which were nothing more than a reflection of themselves (Mark 7:8-9). Indeed, Jesus opposed the institutional authorities of his day because they served up a censored Scripture with easy answers that mirrored their cultural values and norms. You know where this is going.

If Jesus were here now, perhaps our pastors and priests would have the same venomous response. WWRRJD if he stepped off the page and into our churches? Might he again confront the religious authorities, censuring them for their promotion of human traditions instead of God's raw Revelation? Would he chastise them—perhaps with terms like "wicked" and "adulterous"—for offering us an edited and processed Gospel, a censored savior who won't upset our way of thinking and living, instead of the unfiltered truth? Pastors, of course, will not see themselves as analogous to the scribes and Pharisees. Should we expect them to? They have a lot at stake, just like the Jewish leaders did.

So how then do we deal with the real Jesus? There are, of course, many different options. Here is, briefly, what your waiter thinks, the dispensable conclusion.

I relate more to the human Jesus of Matthew, Mark, and Luke than to the divine Christ of John. For me, Jesus is a teacher—go figure that!—who invites me to think, to deepen and stretch my spiritual mind. He challenges my way of living, my view of reality and the world. Right belief about Jesus—whether he was born of a virgin, was fully God and fully human, and so forth—is not nearly as crucial as being in right relationship to Jesus. For me that relationship is as his student. Students listen and learn; they study assiduously; they interact energetically with other pupils. And they also ask questions—hard ones, thoughtful ones—and sometimes they even dissent and argue with the instructor. Good teachers like it when learners do that. Jesus, then, is someone with whom I am free to disagree—a true relationship requires such openness.

So, for example, if we translated many of Jesus' teachings into today's socio-economic terms, it seems to me that Jesus would be a socialist. He opposed the accumulation of wealth and favored its redistribution. When I read the gospels, it is difficult for me to imagine that Jesus would support free market capitalism. But part of me thinks that capitalism, which fundamentally requires people to build bigger barns, is morally defensible and offers some distinct advantages over socialism. I personally am not sure that the accumulation of capital is bad or that sharing it equally with everyone will ultimately result in a good society. But, and here's the key, I don't filter out or water down that aspect of Jesus' message simply because I struggle with it. Rather, I feel free to think-out-loud with Jesus. Like Abraham with God, I am engaged with the issues that Jesus holds before us, in this case the very practical question of how capitalism might fit, or not, with the kingdom of God.

Now maybe you would disagree with my reading of the gospels on this point or my attempt to transmute Jesus' ideas into modern categories. Maybe you would argue that I have created a "disagreement" with Jesus where none exists, namely, that Jesus would not be a socialist. Perhaps you would be right. But you and I would need to have a conversation about the relevant biblical texts. We would need to conduct a reasoned debate — in which I would no doubt suggest that your Adam-Smith Jesus is a reflection of your values rather than the Jesus revealed to us in Scripture, and you would declare that my Karl-Marx Jesus (minus the bad stuff) is a result of my reading too much liberal biblical scholarship. And if we did debate, there's a good chance that both of us would learn something, or see a verse in a new light, or have an original thought, or make an insightful connection; that is, we would have a fresh encounter with Jesus and his teachings. Then we would both be loving God by engaging the Incarnation of God with our minds. And that is what matters.

Jesus is not someone I worship; teachers don't want to be adulated. Not once anywhere in the Gospels does Jesus command that he be praised and honored. In light of his own message about coming to be a servant, to minister to the sick and downtrodden, to wash feet, about the first being last, there is something paradoxical about exalting Jesus. Rather, Jesus inspires me — teachers do want to be inspiring — by holding before me an alternative way of being, specifically, that my life should not revolve around me, that a God-centered life is a life of service to others, that we love God by loving people. It's an unnatural and difficult alternative, one that I do not live out very well. But I am in conversation with Jesus as I struggle along on the journey of faith, haphazardly, amidst life's messiness. Sometimes I take comfort in the idea that Jesus himself struggled with God — recall his cry, "My God, my God, why have you forsaken me?" But many times there is no comfort when I encounter the unedited Jesus of the Gospels — only the stark realization that I am getting a glimpse of God and the life that God calls us to live.

But these are just a few of my thoughts. We must each come to terms with Jesus on our own. And the best ingredients for doing that are reading widely, talking to others, thinking and praying faithfully, and, above all, dining on the raw Gospel.

COURSE 4

DOCTRINE

Our fourth course is a heavier one in the sense that we move from the realm of stories about God and Jesus to the arena of theology and doctrine. We go from narrative to philosophy; and we transition from what the Bible says to what it does not say. The rawness, of course, remains because of the ambiguity and difficulty that we continue to encounter.

Christians typically assume — and you know what they say about assuming — that most of our basic beliefs about God, Jesus, the Holy Spirit, salvation, sacraments, Satan, and the second coming are spelled out lucidly in the Scripture (which, by the way, does not have any edict against alliteration). Preachers tend to bake it that way. But the simple fact is the Bible contains no systematic teaching on any of these subjects. It presents no single, straightforward view on these matters which are so essential to our faith. Church leaders, however, are happy to perpetuate our erroneous assumptions because once we begin to understand the complex history of some of our fundamental tenets, we may have all sorts of new questions. So it's easier to keep feeding us the simple answers in which the complexity has been sifted out.

To be sure, the Bible has been an important element in shaping our beliefs, but it certainly has not been the sole, or even primary, one. That is because the Bible is not a doctrinal treatise. It does not contain the creeds. Men like Origen, Augustine, and Aquinas wrote systematic theological treatises; and Ecumenical Councils like those at Nicea (351 A.D.), Constantinople (381 A.D.) and Chalcedon (451 A.D.) developed the creeds.

The problem is that most Christians don't know much about—or perhaps have never even heard of—these men or these Church Councils. And who can blame them? How exciting can it be to read through page after page of guys named Irenaeus, Tertullian, and Athanasius who are using words like "homoousios"? True, these church fathers go by only one name, which is nice and trendy, but they need better monikers, like Elvis, Beyoncé, or Bono. So since nobody knows about them, it's convenient to pretend that everything we believe is articulated right there in the Bible. But, in fact, many traditional Christian beliefs are only hinted at in Scripture or dealt with indirectly, if at all. Thus it took many arguments and hundreds of years for our tradition to figure out exactly what we believed. To put it generously, many of our basic beliefs are loosely based on the Bible, but like a movie "based on a true story," there is a lot of embellishing, filling in gaps, and creative and imaginative interpretation—which is fine, as long as we recognize that.

Tracing the development of our beliefs deepens our appreciation of our heritage; it helps us see that current teaching is the product of years of tradition, influenced by many different people. It was not handed down from God since the beginning. There has not been one static Christian doctrine or creed from time immemorial. It is not our objective here to trace the historical development of our beliefs. Lucky for you, those discussions can be found in many other good books. Rather, our aim is simply to examine what the Bible says and does not say concerning these core issues.

When we consult the Bible looking for answers about the nature of God, the deity of Christ, the role of the Holy Spirit, the function of the sacraments, the power of Satan, or clues to the apocalypse, we have to pull a verse from here, a short passage from there, one line from a third text, and so on. We must piece it together. It's a precarious task, but it's our only option because the Bible is not a book that methodically addresses these topics. The primary danger that we encounter in this process is proof-texting; that is, taking one or two verses and citing them as proofs to support a specific belief. It's very easy, of course, to quote passages out of context, to use the Bible to bolster whatever belief one wants. As we discovered during the first course of the meal, the Bible is a plus-size book with plenty of different ideas and perspectives in it, so one can locate a couple lines to support just about any position — including the missionary one. Thus we must be cautious.

Our best defense against the onslaught of proof-texting is pretty simple. First, we must take the time to look up the verses cited. Then secondly we need to read the verses that precede and follow it. This might actually require reading the whole chapter — or even the whole book — in which the verses appear. Habakkuk 4:2 exhorts us to do so.

But many times we fail to do these two simple steps, which results in the following sort of scenario: We are curious about a particular subject, so we Google it — say "where is the Trinity in the Bible?" — and numerous websites appear. Many of them make assertions concerning what the Bible says about the Trinity followed by a list of verses as support. We do not take the time to consult the biblical references or we don't read the larger passage in which they are set. We then go on our way assuming that the particular claims have been duly substantiated by the Bible. When we do this, we've been duped, we've eaten the cooked Book.

(handwritten margin note: broad statement)

If, however, we examine the cited verses, and read them in context, then we are taking the time to love God with our minds. In some instances, we will be confused as to how the reference supports the particular doctrinal position. In other cases we will have utterly no idea how the verse even relates to the topic. We will have to make many assumptions, employ odd logic, stretch the obvious sense of the text, or completely ignore the larger context to make it even remotely pertinent to the question. This will not happen in every case of course. But the point is that we must commit to examine the verses in context. A long list of references appears impressive, but it's often just a bunch of hot air. Have you checked Habakkuk 4:2? . . . See what I mean — anybody can say anything and list a reference to support it.

And you thought texting while driving was unsafe. It's proof-texting while theologizing that will get you into some serious doctrinal accidents.

Is God Omni-Everything?

Theology is the study of God's being, nature, and character. The Bible is not a book of systematic theology; rather it is a book which features God as its main character, or at least the main character of the Old Testament who was our main focus in the second course. It might be natural to think that even though God is portrayed in deeply disturbing ways in a variety of passages, there must be other texts which clearly describe the God of classic Christian theology, a God who is omnipresent (present everywhere), omniscient (knows all), omnipotent (all powerful), omnibenevolent (all good), and omnistatic (a word I just made up) — the real final attribute would be immutable (unchangeable). No. Not there. The Bible makes none of these claims. The fundamental attributes of God are not described or defined in Scripture. Yes, the God of the Bible is the source of knowledge, is very powerful, and is not bound by space and time as humans are. But that does not mean he's omni-everything. So what does the Bible say, and not say, about God?

Let's start with the question that my five-year-old son has asked me repeatedly, "Where does God come from?" I tell him I don't know. The Bible does not argue for God's existence; it simple assumes it. It makes no attempt to explain God's origins. The traditional Christian claim that God has always existed is nowhere to be found. The verse which comes closest is Revelation 1:8: "I am the Alpha and the Omega, says the Lord God, who is, and who was, and is to come." Alpha and Omega are the first and last letters of the Greek alphabet, thus God is the beginning and the end, so the reasoning goes. But simply because God created the universe with space and time as we know it does not mean that God has always existed. My son does not buy the notion that God has always been. He staunchly maintains that God, like everyone else, "has been borned."

Concerning God's omnipresence and omniscient, a frequently cited text is Psalm 139. Here the writer claims that God knows each of his actions, thoughts, and words before he speaks them (verses 1-6); thus God is "omniscient." Then he declares that there is no place he can go to escape from God (verses 7-12); thus God is "omnipresent." After a third stanza in which he points out his long standing good relationship with God, the tone abruptly shifts as the writer of the psalm gets down to the business of what he really wants: "O that you would kill the wicked, O God, and that the bloodthirsty would depart from me."

Now, can we really appeal to Psalm 139 as a passage that conveys absolute truths about God's omniscience and omnipresence when it calls on God to kill people? Maybe, if you are a serial killer. But for the rest of us, no. The rhetoric of the psalm as a whole is self-evident: God knows my thoughts and actions; even if I wanted to escape from him, I could not. God has always cared about me, and I am on God's side, so please, God, help me by killing my enemies. This is personal poetry not doctrinal theology.

Here we see a prime example of the problems with proof-texting and the importance of considering the context. The book of Psalms is a collection of songs written by the Israelites and addressed to God. God is not the speaker; rather the Israelites make claims about God and how they experience God. Sometimes they are happy and they praise the deity and say wonderful things about him. Other times they are depressed and angry and express unkind things.

This is why we sampled no texts from Psalms in our consideration of God's character in the earlier course.

Naturally, you never hear the depressing psalms cited in discussion about the attributes of God. For example, here's what Psalm 44 says about the deity: "You have rejected us and abased us" (verse 9). "You have made us like sheep for the slaughter, and have scattered us among the nations" (verse 11). "You have sold your people for a trifle" (verse 12). "You have made us the taunt of our neighbors" (verse 13). "All this has come upon us, yet we have not forgotten you, or been false to your covenant" (verse 17). "Because of you we are being killed all day long, and accounted as sheep for the slaughter" (verse 22). "Rouse yourself! Why do you sleep, O Lord? Awake, do not cast us off forever." Based on this psalm, we must conclude that God is cruel, vindictive, and too sleepy to care.

Or how about Psalm 88 as proof of how much God loves us and hears our prayers: "But I, O Lord, cry out to you; in the morning my prayer comes before you. Lord, why do you ignore me? Why do you hide your face from me? I am wretched and have been close to death from the time of my youth. I suffer your terrors; I am desperate. Your wrath has swept over me; your painful assaults destroy me" (verses 13-16). Why not cite these passages as support for the view that God torments us and neglects us?

In short, people will often reference the psalms when arguing that God is omni-everything. But the Psalms contain a wide variety of statements about the Almighty — including that he is not almighty. It's naïve and disingenuous — to put it mildly — to point to a couple of verses from one psalm as evidence for a particular theological view.

WHAT ABOUT THE TRINITY?

The doctrine of the Trinity states that God is one being, but is manifested in three persons: the Father, the Son, and the Holy Spirit. The word "Trinity," however, does not appear anywhere in the Bible. That's not surprising perhaps. But even the idea is hard find. Nowhere does it say, "God is three persons in one" or "God is triune." It never uses the number three when talking about God. It does not compare God to a tricycle, a triangle, or a trifecta. The closest we come are verses which mention God, Jesus, and the Spirit, such as Matthew 28:19: "Therefore go and make disciples of all nations, baptizing them in the name of the Father and of the Son and of the Holy Spirit." Or 2 Corinthians 13:14: "May the grace of the Lord Jesus Christ, and the love of God, and the fellowship of the Holy Spirit be with you all." Also, the Gospel of John, by far the best single place for Trinitarian ideas, features a couple of instances in which Jesus talks about the Father sending the Spirit in Jesus' name (John 14:26 and 15:26). If Jesus himself were aware of his being one-third of the Godhead, he's got plenty of good opportunities to say so in John, but this is as close as he gets.

In the vast majority of times in Scripture only one of the three is mentioned or perhaps two — Jesus and God — which is especially notable in places where you'd expect to find all three. Take the well-known John 1:1 for example: "In the beginning was the Word, and the Word was with God and the Word was God." Here we've got God the Father and Jesus the Son (the Word) clearly defined as divine and seemingly equal. But what about the Holy Spirit — what better place to introduce it and its role? Absent. Two out of three ain't bad, but it ain't the Trinity.

It is true that God, Jesus, and the Holy Spirit are major players in the New Testament; but fundamental questions about how the three relate to one another, how their source and being are connected, or whether all three are equally divine are never answered. Thus the Church Councils debated these issues at length and did not develop the doctrine of the Trinity as we know it today until more than 300 years after the death of Jesus.

There is one other sticking point here—the Old Testament. The Israelite creed is abundantly clear: "Hear O Israel, the Lord our God, the Lord is one!" The Jews have never had a belief in a triune God. It's strictly a Christian concept. When we are directed to Old Testament passages that purportedly support a Trinitarian view, we must read them with exclusively Christian eyes—which is perfectly acceptable, as long as we realize that we are doing so. For example, Christians commonly point out that the word for God in Hebrew (Elohim) is plural in form or that God says "Let us [plural] make humankind in our image." When Christians go looking for the Trinity in the Jewish Scripture, this is what they find—some vague hints at plurality, which could mean two gods or two hundred. But that does not change the fact that the writers of the Old Testament, like the Jews to this day, viewed God as singular, one—not three in one. God may have existed in the beginning, but the notion of the Trinity did not.

IS GOD A BOY OR A GIRL?

Let's consider one other question concerning the nature of God. According to the Bible, does God have a physical body, and if so, is God male or female? The Old Testament features numerous anthropomorphic images of God — places where God is depicted in human-like terms: walking in the Garden, breathing into the mouth of humans, smelling sacrifices, speaking with a thunderous voice, stretching out his hand, writing with his finger, and talking with Moses face-to-face regularly. If we take these passages literally — and based on the context in which they appear, there is no obvious reason not to — then one could reasonably argue that God, at least the God of the Old Testament, has a physical body.

Most Christians, of course, read these passages meta-phorically, not literally. They can also cite John 4:24, among others, which states that God is a spirit. So if God does not have a body, then God cannot be male or female, right? God does not have testicles or a vagina? So why then do Christians tend to think of God as male, refer to God with the masculine pronoun (he), and address God as Father? Some possible responses are that the Old Testament refers to God in the masculine, Jesus referred to God as Father, and Jesus himself was God and he was a man — that is, God was incarnated in the flesh of a man not a woman. So does that mean God is a man? Does God, then, have a penis? Or does only one-third of the Godhead (Jesus) have a penis? And if God has a penis, is it circumcised (okay, I shouldn't joke about circumcision)?

But if God is a spirit, and does not have a body, then is God a male spirit? And what in the world would "male spirit" mean? Can you be bodiless and still be male? Would you then have a spiritual penis?

As is evident, it can get quite complicated and the Bible doesn't offer much clarity. To further muddy the waters, the Old Testament does occasionally use feminine language to describe God. Genesis 1:2 — just the second verse in the whole Bible — says the "spirit of God" hovered over the face of the waters. The Hebrew word rendered "spirit" is a feminine noun. Later in Genesis 1, both male and female are created in the image of God. Isaiah 42:14 and 49:15 apply feminine imagery to God, namely, God as a woman in labor and as a mother nursing her child. So is God a woman? Can we really say that these feminine depictions are "just symbolic," but "God as Father" is literal? It makes total sense to me, by *funny* the way, that God would be a woman, for it explains why I've never figured out what God wants. It also accounts for the command, "Thou shalt not commit adultery." No guy would have ever come up with that. ☺

In brief (not "briefs"), the Bible is not clear as to whether God has a body or if God is male or female or neither, or if those are even the correct categories. These may sound like silly questions, but let's face it, they are relatively basic. We should give some thought to what it means to believe in a bodiless God, and yet refer to that God as Father, as opposed to Mother or something else. Indeed, the pronouns we use to talk about God are of fundamental importance for how we relate to him ... uh, I mean, God.

WHO DID JESUS THINK HE WAS?

Enough about God. Who is Jesus? Who did Jesus himself claim to be? And who did the New Testament writers claim him to be? These are three related, but separate, questions. Our answer to the first question — Who is Jesus? — should be based primarily on the answers to the second and third if we want our views to be grounded in Scripture, rather than on the flavored images of Jesus we find elsewhere.

So let's start with the second query: Who did Jesus himself think he was? When we read the first three gospels, we don't find one place where Jesus claims to be God or even the Son of God. He may have thought of himself as the Son of Man, and he claims the power to forgive sins, which the Jewish leaders say only God can do; but strikingly absent is a clear claim to divinity. In fact, there are places where he suggests just the opposite, such as when he asks the rich man, "Why do you call me good? No one is good but God alone" (Mark 10:18; Luke 18:19). Even in the Gospel of John, Jesus himself never claims to be God in the flesh; though he suggests his divine status with statements like, "Before Abraham was, I am" (John 8:58) and "My father and I are one" (John 10:30), or "The father is in me and I am in my father" (John 10:38). Jesus also makes confusing statements in John, such as in 14:28, "The Father is greater than I," suggesting that even if he is God, he is not equal with God. (This, incidentally, is also a good memory verse for your children.)

Jesus himself, of course, did not write the Gospels, so when we ask "who did Jesus claim to be" we are dependent on what the gospel writers tell us, the words they put in the mouth of Jesus. In those words, Jesus does not claim to be God. This fact strongly suggests that Jesus did not think of himself as divine. Let's ruminate on that for a minute: It is difficult to imagine Jesus making such an assertion about himself and not one gospel writer bothering to include it one time.

Who, then, did the New Testament writers claim Jesus to be (the third question)? Did they say that he was God? They frequently call him the Son of God, the Son of Man, the Messiah, and Lord, but this is not tantamount to calling him God (Greek: theos). A few texts, however, do say he was

God. The aforementioned John 1:1, for instance, declares, "In the beginning was the Word [Jesus] and the Word was with God and the Word was God." Several other texts come fairly close. Colossians 1:15 says that Jesus "is the image of the invisible God and in 1:19 it states that, "In him all the fullness of God was pleased to dwell." Likewise Colossians 2:9 says, "For in him the whole fullness of deity dwells bodily." Other passages which are usually mentioned in this discussion include Romans 9:5; 2 Thessalonians 1:12; Titus 2:13; and 2 Peter 1:1. So while the New Testament does assert that Jesus is God, it does so on only a few occasions, about as often as it condemns sexual relations with your step mother (1 Corinthians 5).

The New Testament's reticence on this subject is presumably the result of a strong monotheism—belief in one God. It was only with time, probably about one hundred years after his death, that people were comfortable with calling Jesus God. Like the concept of the Trinity, belief in the divinity of Jesus developed slowly. As with Jimmy Carter, Jesus' reputation improved substantially with time.

Perhaps you've heard someone say: Jesus was either Lord, a liar, or a lunatic. It's quite a clever ploy because it only gives you three options and no one will choose the second or third. Therefore Jesus must be Lord/God. But that is like asking you: Is your favorite color magenta, teal, or saffron? There are other possibilities of course. The most obvious one—with Jesus, not the colors—is that Jesus did not claim to be Lord God, in which case he was neither Lord, nor a liar, nor or a lunatic. So the answer would be D, none of the above. Never let people color you into a corner with sneaky questions.

WHO'S ON THIRD?

The Holy Spirit is a tough one to discern, which is not surprising since its other name is Holy Ghost. Its role, function, purpose, and relationship to Jesus the Son and God the Father are not clearly addressed — nor is its degree of friendliness. First off, the Holy Spirit does not appear in the Old Testament, which of course makes sense since the Israelites had no concept of the Trinity. (Remember, when you read the Old Testament with Christian lenses, you can find whatever you want.) Rather, the belief in a Holy Spirit emerged over time, namely with the coming of Jesus and the early church.

A particularly vexing question concerns the timing of the arrival of the Holy Spirit. The New Testament is thoroughly confusing on this point. In John 16:5-15, Jesus says to his disciples that the Holy Spirit will come *after* Jesus has returned to the Father. It actually says that the "Helper" or "Comforter" or "Advocate" will come — the Greek is Paraclete — but this refers to the Holy Spirit, as John 14:5 makes evident. The same idea is found in John 7:39 and Acts 1:3-5 — the Holy Spirit will not arrive until Jesus departs. This scenario plays out at Pentecost in Acts 2 when the Holy Spirit makes its dramatic appearance after Jesus has ascended to heaven. So far so good — it even fits with the fact that the Holy Spirit is not in the Old Testament. If someone, then, claims to find the Holy Spirit in the Old Testament, they'll have to explain that to Jesus.

But wait a minute. The Holy Spirit has already appeared during the life of Jesus. John the Baptist and his mother Elizabeth are filled with the Holy Spirit (Luke 1:15 and 1:41), as are Zechariah (Luke 1:67) and Simeon (Luke 2:25). The Holy Spirit impregnates Mary (Luke 1:35). Don't ask how. It descends on Jesus at his baptism in the form of a dove (Luke 3:22; Matthew 3:16; Mark 1:10), which makes the Mary scene all the more, shall we say, perplexing. According to Jesus, the Spirit can be obtained any time merely by asking (Luke 11:13). Furthermore, after his resurrection but before his ascension Jesus gives the Holy Spirit to his disciples (John 20:22). What is going on here? This is not some obscure discrepancy, nor one that can be easily reconciled. No, these are inconsistent assertions about a major issue: one-third of the Godhead. Which is not very comforting for someone called the Great Comforter.

It is refreshing, though, to have a Holy Ghost in our tradition even if it means we can't assure our children that "ghosts aren't real."

ARE YOU SAVED? *pushing it*

Christians have more-or-less adhered to the same basic set of beliefs about God, the Trinity, and Jesus — the Bible's lack of clarity not withstanding — but this cannot be said about salvation, which various groups have understood quite differently. These differences are due in large part to the complexity and ambiguity of Scripture, which Christians would do well to acknowledge. For example, the language of "asking Jesus into your heart" or "praying to accept Jesus as your personal savior" is not found in the Bible. Not one time. Likewise, the Bible does not say anything anywhere about the salvation of children or about babies going to heaven when they die. There is nothing about an age of accountability or anything of the sort. But Scripture does tell us that women can be saved through childbearing — if they live with faith, love, holiness, and modesty (1 Timothy

2:15). Thus there is more biblical support for the salvation of virtuous mothers than of infants. And this is just the beginning.

Let's chew on the famous John 3:16 for a moment to demonstrate how convoluted this topic can be: "For God so loved the world that he gave his only begotten son that whosoever believes in him should not perish but have everlasting life." Despite the fact that Christians often think of this verse as a straightforward presentation of the Gospel message, a number of questions quickly arise when we take a minute to consider what it says, and does not say. Next time you see someone holding a John 3:16 sign, here are a few of the queries you might pose to them.

What does it mean to "believe in him (Jesus)"? How do I show that I believe—do I simply have to say something or must I do something as well? Does it mean to believe his teachings and do them? Or does it mean to believe that he lived and died and was resurrected? Or does it mean to believe that his death paid for my sins and placated God's punishment that was coming to me? What is so "loving" about God sending his son to die—couldn't God just forgive us without requiring his own Son to be killed? What does killing one's own Son have to do with loving the world? So maybe the phrase "gave his Son" has nothing to do with death and payment for sins—maybe he "gave his Son" in order to bring the kingdom of God to humankind, to show us how to live and love one another? What about "should not perish but have everlasting life"? So if I don't believe— whatever it means to believe—then I perish, I die a physical death and that's it? It doesn't say anything about going to hell. And besides, going to hell isn't perishing, is it? And if I do believe in Jesus, does that mean I never die? Of course my body will die, so it must mean my soul will live forever; but I thought the New Testament said that everyone has a soul that lives forever. Then what's the big deal about "not perishing" and having "everlasting life"? So maybe it means I have everlasting life with God as opposed to everlasting death? If so, is "everlasting life" the same thing as going to heaven? But why doesn't the verse mention heaven? Or is "everlasting life" a state of being rather than a place? If it's a place, where is it and what does it look like? If it's a state of being, when can I enter it and how do I maintain it? And if this is just my soul living eternally, does that mean I'll have no physical body?

Whew. Maybe next time, they'll think twice about holding up the John 3:16 sign. Or maybe they'll choose another verse.

If we apply a similar degree of rigor to each passage of the New Testament that deals with salvation, it's easy to see how the confusion can multiply quickly. In light of the potential quagmire, let's limit ourselves to one issue: Regardless of exactly what salvation is, how does one obtain it?

It depends on whom you ask. Paul, James, and Jesus essentially have different answers. Paul's is the simplest and easiest, and so, not coincidentally, it is the most popular. Paul focuses almost exclusively on the significance of the death of Jesus, which is a compelling fact in itself. Paul says next to nothing about the birth, teachings, and miracles of Jesus that we read about in the Gospels. For Paul, humans have sinned (Romans 3:23) and the penalty for sin is death (Romans 6:23). Jesus died in order to pay the penalty for our sins (Romans 5:8). If "you confess with your mouth that Jesus is Lord and believe in your heart that God raised him from the dead, you will be saved" (Romans 10:9). That's it. Pretty easy. "Since we have been justified through faith, we have peace with God through our Lord Jesus Christ" (Romans 5:1). Faith, and faith alone, is all that is required for salvation — salvation from death and the wrath of God's judgment. (See also Galatians 2:16 and Ephesians 2:8-9.)

James sees things a bit differently, as has been long recognized. James says that "faith by itself, if it has no works, is dead" (2:17). That is, for James, you got to do stuff; faith alone doesn't cut it. If we read James 2:14-26, we can see how his view flies in the face of Paul's. Their divergences can best be seen by how each one interprets the story of Abraham. Paul argues that Abraham was justified by faith, not by works: "If Abraham was justified by works, he has something to boast about, but not before God. For what does the Scripture say? 'Abraham believed God, and it was reckoned to him as righteousness'" (Romans 4:2). For Paul, Abraham's belief was enough.

James, in sharp contrast, writes, "Was not our father Abraham considered righteous for what he did when he offered his son Isaac on the altar? You see that his faith and his actions were working together, and his faith was made complete by what he did." Accordingly, "You see that a person is considered righteous by what they do and not by faith alone" (2:21-24). In case we don't recall the stories of Abraham, James gives a second, sexier example: Rahab the prostitute from Jericho who was saved by her tricks. No, not those tricks. But by hiding the Israelite spies and helping them escape secretly (James 2:25). She too is justified by her works, not faith alone. Paul and James agree that one must have faith. They disagree, however, on whether faith is sufficient for salvation.

So what are these "works" that we must perform according to James? You must pray five times a day, give alms, fast, and make a pilgrimage to . . . Oh wait, wrong religion. Seriously, you must pray (though not five times a day), go to church faithfully, give money regularly, be a loyal employee, and love your family. So fortunately, most of us are good to go.

Not.

I highly recommend reading all of James — it's packed with wisdom — so you can see for yourself what "works" we must do. But I can quote several items for you: "Suppose a brother or a sister is without clothes and food. If one of you says to them, 'Go in peace; keep warm and well fed,' but does nothing about their physical needs, what good is that? Likewise, faith alone, if it is not accompanied by action, is dead" (2:15-17). Or "Religion that God our Father accepts as pure and faultless is this: to care for orphans and widows in their distress and to keep oneself from being polluted by the world" (1:27). If you are looking for orphans and widows to care for, there are many of them in Sub-Saharan Africa, India, and China, not to mention a few in your own zip code.

So, are you saved, according to James?

Preachers may try to harmonize Paul and James by asserting that James is claiming that if one's faith is genuine, it will manifest itself with good works. Maybe so. But at least one smart guy named Martin Luther did not think they could be reconciled, so he wanted to throw James out of the Bible. While Luther was at it, he should have tossed out Jesus too since, according to Jesus, there are no free lunches, or faith-only salvations.

There is no passage in the Gospels where Jesus proclaims — or the narrator or anyone at all, for that matter — that one needs to believe in Jesus' death and resurrection for the forgiveness of sins in order to receive salvation or eternal life. In other words, there is nothing that sounds remotely like Paul. Yes, there are a couple of texts in which Jesus suggests that his death is a sacrificial atonement (Mark 10:45; Matthew 26:28). But it's not mentioned in connection with the terms faith, belief, salvation, or eternal life. There are also a handful of verses in John, such as 3:16, which indicate that belief in Jesus leads to eternal life (3:36, 6:40 and maybe 6:47 and 17:3). But, again, there is nothing in these passages about having faith in his death and resurrection for salvation. If Jesus himself understood the crucifixion in the same way as Paul and other New Testament writers, it's virtually inconceivable that he would not make this clear at least once. But he doesn't.

If you recall our course on Jesus, you already know what he says about salvation. It's quite like James — and not good for most of us. A rich man asks Jesus, "What must I do to inherit eternal life?" (Mark 10:17-22; Matthew 19:16-22; Luke 18:18-25). In the same story, the disciples ask Jesus, "Who then can be saved?" thus equating the terms "eternal life" and "salvation." So then according to Jesus, what is the formula for salvation? Oh come on, you remember. That's right: keep the Jewish law, specifically the Ten Commandments, and sell all that you own and give the money to the poor.

Can we as Christians, with a straight face, dilute the words of Jesus by arguing that Jesus' answer only applied until the time of his death, and Paul's view holds thereafter? Do we really have the audacity to say, "Now that Jesus has been crucified and raised, we are reconciled to God; thus we don't need to worry about anything that Jesus himself says regarding salvation and eternal life"? Even if we'd like to try that, Matthew 25:31-46 won't let us. We've already gotten a taste of this text as well.

This passage is particularly compelling because, unlike the others, it smacks of the final judgment—it's not Jesus talking to one rich man in one time and place. Instead, it begins: "When the Son of Man comes in his glory, and all the angels with him, then he will sit on the throne of his glory. All the nations will be gathered before him, and he will separate people one from another as a shepherd separates the sheep from the goats." This is the dramatic moment of truth for everyone. The sheep who "inherit the kingdom prepared for you from the foundation of the world" and "eternal life" are those who feed the hungry, give drink to the thirsty, welcome strangers, clothe the naked, take care of the sick, and visit those in prison. The goats who are "accursed" and sent "into the eternal fire prepared for the devil and his angels" and receive "eternal punishment" are those who do not minister to the needs "of the least of these." Again, how to inherit eternal life and avoid eternal punishment is laid out quite unmistakably. And this time it's the final judgment, after Jesus has died, and the teaching remains consistent: Care for those in need.

Even the Gospel of John, despite its ideas on belief in the Son for eternal life, contains a similar passage about earning salvation. John 5:28-29 describes Jesus, the "Son of Man," executing judgment: "The hour is coming when all who are in their graves will hear his voice and will come out—those who have done good, to the resurrection of life, and those who have done evil, to the resurrection of the condemnation." Jesus does not outline specifically what qualifies as having "done good" or "done evil," but eternal life clearly involves more than just belief. One can see why John 3:16 is more popular than John 5:28-29 even though, frankly, the latter is probably more straightforward. For Jesus, salvation is not a "free gift."

Despite the lack of clarity in the New Testament about salvation and how one obtains it, we can conclude with some confidence based on the Gospel record that Jesus himself — quite unlike Paul — did not view faith in his death and resurrection as the way to salvation and eternal life. Instead, according to Jesus, and James, it is acquired through doing good works on behalf of the poor, suffering, and oppressed.

WHAT THE HECK?

Not only is Scripture unclear on what salvation is and how one obtains it, but it's also ambiguous on what we are saved from. For many Christians — though certainly not all — we are saved from hell, a place of eternal fire and torment. Remarkably, the Bible never says that. It says many other things, like salvation is from sin (Matthew 1:21; 1 Timothy 1:14), from death (James 5:20), from God's wrath (Romans 5:9), and from the present evil age (Galatians 1:4) of Paris Hilton and Kim Kardashian. But never from hell. Likewise, nowhere does the Bible say that being saved means going to heaven. Nowhere does it connect the idea of salvation with heaven. For some Christians this is the heart of the Gospel message: Trust in Jesus as your savior so you will go to heaven when you die instead of hell. Yet it cannot be found in one place in Scripture.

Maybe, we might speculate, the Bible does not explicitly assert that salvation is from hell because everybody already knew that—it would have been so obvious that Jesus or Paul did not need to say it. Actually, quite the opposite is the case. Judaism at the time had no concept of a literal place of eternal punishment. Hell is not found in the Old Testament. The word Sheol appears 65 times there, usually translated "pit" or "grave," but sometimes as "hell." Sheol is not a place of everlasting suffering; rather it's the underworld, the realm of the dead, a place of rest for the deceased. See, for example, Genesis 37:35; Job 14:13; Proverbs 9:18; Psalm 16:10; 89:48; and 139:8 (this last one is especially illustrative, because if Sheol is hell, God is there). The Old Testament, accordingly, has no notion of heaven either. In fact, there is no belief in an afterlife in the Jewish Scripture—though there may be hints of it in the book of Daniel. Like many other doctrines, heaven and hell are ideas which evolve slowly over the course of the history of our tradition.

If the Old Testament contains no concept of a place of eternal torment from which to be saved, what about hell in the New Testament? Hell is a translation of the Greek word *gehenna*, which appears a mere twelve times, not a particularly hot topic, you might say. *Gehenna* was the name of a specific place, namely, the garbage dump outside Jerusalem where trash burned continually. Hence "fire" and *gehenna* were closely associated (e.g., Matthew 5:22; 18:9; Mark 9:43, 45). Further, it was a fire that was always burning; thus Jesus refers to the "eternal fire" of *gehenna*.

Given that *gehenna*/hell was a known location, it would seem natural to conclude that Jesus and the New Testament writers used the term *gehenna* metaphorically—they did not mean that someone was literally going to the trash pile. Rather, *gehenna* was a symbol of destruction. Those who did not join the kingdom, Jesus warned, were destined for dumpy, unfulfilled lives of pain and suffering, weeping and gnashing of teeth.

So who exactly is "going to *gehenna*/hell"? Not once in the Bible is hell a place for those who do not "accept Jesus" or believe in his death on the cross as payment for their sins. It's for people who say, "You fool" (Matthew 5:22), for those who continue lusting with their eyes and yet refuse to gouge them out (Matthew 5:29; 18:9) or who keep sinning with their hand or their foot and do not cut it off (Matthew 5:30; Mark 9:45); it is for the hypocrites like the scribes and Pharisees (Matthew 23:13-15). That's raw stuff—regardless of whether you take hell literally or metaphorically—because most of us fall into one or more of those groups. The highway to hell is going to be crowded.

What about the book of Revelation—isn't hell talked about there? No. The word *gehenna* does not appear in Revelation. What does appear is the "lake of fire"—a grand total of five times over the course of only three chapters (19:20; 20:10; 20:14; 20:15; 21:8). Nowhere, then, does the New Testament explicitly connect "hell" and the "lake of fire," even though many Christians routinely assume they are the same thing. Who then, according to the Bible, is thrown into the lake of fire? The beast, the false prophet, the Devil, Death and Hades, anyone whose name was not found written in the book of life, and those who are cowards, faithless, polluted, murderers, fornicators, sorcerers, idolaters, and liars. As with *gehenna*, the focus here is on what you do, not what you believe; you will be sent to the lake of fire for your actions, which is too bad since a lot of us are cowards, fornicators, or liars—sometimes all three at once. But, hey, the good news is that you don't have to help the poor.

In sum, the notion that hell is a lake of fire of eternal torment for those who do not believe in Jesus is not found anywhere in the New Testament. Nowhere does the Bible say that to be saved means being saved from hell. And nowhere does it refer to hell's kitchen as the place where people cook the Good Book.

WHERE DID SATAN COME FROM?

The Bible features a number of spiritual beings — the angel of the Lord, sons of God, a heavenly court, Satan, the Devil, demons, even ghosts. But their identity, nature, appearance, origin, powers, and purpose are difficult to determine. There is certainly no clear biblical teaching about such beings.

Satan, or the Devil, basically appears only in the New Testament. The writers of the Old Testament had no such belief in a personified evil being. The concept of a demonic force developed in Jewish thinking as a result of contact with Persian religion three or four hundred years before Jesus, that is, after most of the Old Testament was written. It is only in some of the latest texts of the Old Testament that Satan shows up (1 Chronicles 21:1, Job 1-2, and Zechariah 3:1-2). By the time of Christianity, a number of religions in the Middle East had developed belief in some sort of malevolent force which opposed the powers of good; hence the Christian concept of the Devil. When we realize that our religious tradition did not originally believe in Satan's existence, but only gradually developed such a belief, we might begin to think about Satan a bit differently. In general, though, it's best not to think about Satan at all.

So let's make one other quick point and then put Satan behind us. The story that Satan and his angels rebelled against God and were expelled from heaven is not in the Bible. If you do some research on this, you will usually end up in Isaiah 14, as that is as close as anyone can get. But it only takes a minute to realize this chapter has absolutely nothing to do with Satan. Isaiah 14 taunts the downfall of the King of Babylon; see verse 4. Verses 12-15 describe him, the enemy king, as "fallen from heaven, O Day Star, son of Dawn." The Latin translation of Day Star is Lucifer, which is why Satan is sometimes referred to as such. If we keep reading the chapter, it is obvious that the referent is a human king, perhaps Sargon II or Sennacherib. I suspect some of you will argue that it refers to Sargon I, not the II. But the fact remains: it has nothing to do with Satan and his angels.

Or maybe you are thinking of the Nephilim in Genesis 6 as a possible reference to "fallen angles." Genesis 6:1-4 is a bizarre text that has baffled commentators. It evidently has something to do with divine beings — the sons of God and the Nephilim — having sexual relations with human women and producing giant offspring. If the Niphilim are "fallen angels," then we should observe that they are hanging out with the "sons of God," a phrase often rendered "angels" in other passages (as in good, normal angels with wings and halos). Moreover, the Niphilim and "sons of God" can impregnate you — if you are a woman. The belief that Christians have protective guardian angels watching over them has nary a shred of biblical support. If, however, one believes that angels can have intercourse with women, there is clear Scriptural backing in Genesis 6, as well as the virgin Mary story.

Paul may have believed it too. Take a look at 1 Corinthians 11:10, another passage that has confounded interpreters. Here women are commanded to pray with their heads covered "because of the angels." Some have suggested that the peculiar phrase "because of the angels" is best understood as a reference to supernatural beings who might look lustfully on women, like the ones in Genesis 6. Hence women should be modest and cover themselves. This gives the phrase "guardian angel" a creepy new meaning.

WHAT'S THE ORDER OF SERVICE?

The Bible does not have much to say about the church, and what it does say is hardly germane to today's body of believers. There are no instructions in the Bible about meeting on Sundays, mid-week prayer meetings, the order of service, how to conduct the Lord's Supper and baptisms, the attire of priests or preachers, the nature of the music, which pre-school curriculum to use, or if there should be a singles group. Many of our customs and traditions developed slowly, long after the New Testament was written. And they developed rather differently. The contrasts between, say, a Southern Baptist church and New England Episcopal one, or an Evangelical Pentecostal service and Roman Catholic Mass, are so great that they are barely recognizable as being the same religion—and in some cases barely recognizable as religion at all. As we venture around the globe, the differences are even more pronounced.

The practices of and instructions given to the New Testament church are rather foreign to our way of thinking. For example, if we followed the early Christians, we would condone slavery. Paul writes a whole book to a "dear friend and co-worker" who is also a slave owner, Philemon, concerning his slave Onesimus. Not once does Paul challenge or question the institution of slavery. Similarly, Christian slaves are enjoined to be submissive to their masters (Titus 2:9-10; 1 Peter 2:18-25). The New Testament's acceptance of slavery is hard to swallow given the notion that Scripture is inspired. Furthermore, during worship services, women (as we just noted) were to have a veil or covering on their head when they prayed or prophesied, while men were to have their head uncovered (1 Corinthians 11:4-5). It was disgraceful for a man to have long hair, which was only fitting for a woman, and perhaps served as her covering or veil (1 Corinthians 11:14-15). Women also were "to dress themselves modestly and decently in suitable clothing, not with their hair braided, or with gold, pearls, or expensive clothes" (1Timothy 2:8-9). Women also were to "learn in silence with full submission." They were "not to teach or to have authority over a man" but were "to keep silent" and were "not permitted to speak" in church. If they wanted to know something, they were to ask their husbands at home. "For it is shameful for a woman to speak in church" (1 Corinthians 14:34-35; 1 Timothy 2:11-12).

Preachers tend to dismiss these sorts of texts by arguing that such instructions applied only to the original audience — they were relevant for only one specific time and place. They are not permanent commands, so the thinking goes. The problem with that, as you well know, is that we can make the same argument concerning any biblical passage that we personally dislike. Anything we find unpalatable can be written off with, "Oh, well, that was only back then." Pastors also candy coat these texts by proposing that we are to glean only the principle of the matter — modesty, humility, and mutual submission — not the specific commands about gold, braided hair, and silence of women. Again, anyone is free to make that claim with any portion of Scripture that doesn't fit their tastes. And besides, do we really live by the principles: I have seen more skin in churches than in nightclubs. Not that I was looking.

Now a word about the sacraments: Baptism and the Eucharist (or Lord's Supper or Communion). It can be brief because there is very little detailed discussion of them anywhere in the New Testament. Baptism was not unique to the early Christians, as we can tell from the fact that John is baptizing prior to Jesus (e.g., John 1:28). There is nothing about infant baptism — or infant dedication, for that matter — in the New Testament. Christians did, however, baptize on behalf of the dead, a practice which Paul seemingly condoned (1 Corinthians 15:29). Thus there is more Scriptural support for performing a baptism for your deceased grandmother than for baptizing your baby.

Concerning the Eucharist, the Bible does not address the question of whether we are partaking of the literal body and blood of Christ — the Catholic doctrine of Transubstantiation — or if it is strictly symbolic. Nor, by the way, did Jesus say "Bite me," or "Eat me" at the Last Supper. But he did come pretty close in John 6:53-54: "Truly I tell you, unless you eat the flesh of the Son of Man and drink his blood, you have no life in you. Whoever eats my flesh and drinks my blood has eternal life, and I will raise them up at the last day." That's, literally, a raw means to salvation. It also explains why early Christians were sometimes thought to be cannibals (which is true — not that they were, but that people thought they were).

In 1 Corinthians 11 Paul admonishes believers for abusing the Lord's Supper. Apparently it had become something of a huge party in which poorer members were left out. Paul

exhorts people to examine themselves carefully before partaking. If you don't, you "drink judgment on yourselves.
That is why many among you are weak and sick, and a
number of you have died." Now there is a theodicy—an
explanation for why bad things happen—that you don't
hear in church these days: You are ill with cancer because
God is punishing you for taking Communion carelessly.
But it's biblical.

How Much Money Should I Give?

Let's consider one other church-related issue which is
a major focus in some denominations today: giving ten
percent of your income (the tithe) to the church. Tithing
is strictly an Old Testament concept; there is no command
anywhere in the New Testament to donate a percentage of
money to the church. Christians obviously do not follow
the Jewish laws, yet preachers do not hesitate to cite the
commands to tithe as though they were still authoritative,
even as they ignore all the other Old Testament laws. To be
frank, it's a selfishly selective use—and abuse—of the Bible.
It's the Scripture burnt to a crisp. Not only is there nothing
in the New Testament about tithing, but even a survey of
the Old Testament passages proves rather surprising.

Preachers sometimes quote Genesis 14 where Abram—or
Abraham—gives one-tenth of the booty (always a fun word
to say) that he has captured in war to King Melchizedek,
a priest of God. This shows, the argument goes, that even
though we no longer follow the Jewish laws, tithing is still
binding on Christians because Abraham tithed, and he lived
before the laws were given. Oooh, clever. Sounds reasonable,
until we actually look at the text. In the story, Abraham goes

to war to rescue the inhabitants of Sodom—yes, the same Sodom that God will destroy a few chapters later—where his nephew Lot is living. After the battle, Abraham offers ten percent of the spoils of war to Melchizedek, and the rest, that would be the other ninety percent, he returns to the king and people of Sodom. Abraham himself gets nothing. If this story has anything to do with Christians today continually (not one time as Abraham did) giving ten percent of their earned monetary income (not the spoils of war) to the church (not one priest), then we need to be sure to donate the other ninety percent of our money to whatever we deem to be the modern day Sodom—say, your local strip club.

Jacob's tithing practices are ones that we aren't likely to hear discussed in a sermon. In Genesis 28:20-22 Jacob makes a vow saying, "If God will be with me, and [if God] will protect me on my journey, and [if God] will give me bread to eat, and clothing to wear . . . then the Lord shall be my God . . . and of all that you give me I will surely give one-tenth to you." For Jacob, tithing was contingent on God first blessing him, an idea which runs counter to everything we hear from today's preachers who declare that if we first tithe, then God will bless us. Jacob wasn't taking any chances; he demanded the material gain first.

So much for stories. What about the actual laws regarding tithing? Deuteronomy 12:1-19 discusses tithes, gifts, and offerings which are to be brought to the temple. What was to be done with this grain, wine, oil, and the firstlings of the herds and flocks? Answer: "These you shall eat in the presence of the Lord your God . . . you together with your son and your daughter, your male and female slaves, and the Levites from your towns, rejoicing in the presence of the Lord your God in all your undertakings" (verse 18).

That's right, the law instructs that the tithes be used for a block party. It did not go to the Levites (the religious leaders), the temple/church, or to the foreign mission fund. The one who brought the tithe ate it as part of celebration unto God.

The exact same instructions are given again in Deuteronomy 14:22-27, with two notable additions. Here it states that if the temple is too far away to transport one's tithes (animals, grain, etc.), one may exchange the tithe for money, bring the money to the temple and "spend the money for whatever you wish — oxen, sheep, wine, strong drink, or whatever you desire. And you shall eat there in the presence of the Lord your God." Money, then, was not an acceptable tithe — only physical goods, including "strong drink." God evidently does not accept cash. The second addition is found in verses 28-30 which command that every third year, "the tithe of your produce" — again, no money is allowed — is to be stored in one's hometown for the priests. But, alas, even that is not strictly for the clergy. It was also "for the resident aliens, the orphans, and the widows in your towns." So the priests would get only one portion of one-tenth of the produce every three years. For those scoring at home, that averages out to less than three percent a year. Deuteronomy 26 repeats these commands.

Ordinances concerning tithing also appear in Leviticus 27:30-33 and Numbers 18:21-24. In the former text, "All tithes from the land, whether the seed from the ground or the fruit from the tree, are the Lord's; they are to be holy to the Lord." Likewise for animals: "All tithes of the herd and flock, every tenth one that passes under the shepherd's staff, is be holy to the Lord." Here the tithes go directly to God, not the priests, which means the tithes are burned or poured out on the altar as a sacrifice. That is tantamount to collecting the tithe money and then lighting it on fire. It is not used for anything practical. "Giving it to the Lord" means only God is the recipient—no one else benefits, which makes perfect sense when you think about it. Who benefits from your tithe?

Tithing is mentioned a time or two in the New Testament, though it is never ordered. In Matthew 23:23 and Luke 11:42 Jesus chastises the scribes and the Pharisees for tithing, but yet disregarding the "weighty matters of the law: justice, mercy, and faith." He then says that they should practice the latter without neglecting the former (tithing). It thus can be rightly said that Jesus advocated tithing. But then again, he also advocated following all 613 of the other Old Testament laws. Actually, Jesus said that if we wanted to be his disciple, we must sell all that we have and give the money to the poor. That's 100 percent. Preachers probably figure that's too much to ask.

WHEN WILL IT END?

Unlike some of the other topics addressed so far, many Christians are probably already aware of just how confusing the Bible is when it comes to the end times. If even our preachers have the good sense to admit that it's not clear, imagine just how bewildering it must be. We will also find here that proof-texting is at a premium. People pick one verse from Revelation, one from Daniel, another from Mark 13. Factor in the bizarre imagery and symbolism in these books and it's an utter free-for-all. To avoid getting lost in the fray, let's look at only two issues: the rapture and heaven.

The word "rapture" does not appear in the Bible. The idea — popularized by certain recent books and movies — that Christians will leave the earth and meet the returning Jesus in the clouds is based primarily on 1 Thessalonians 4:13-18. In this passage, Paul addresses the question of what happens to believers who die before Christ returns. Paul taught the early believers that Jesus was coming back very soon — within their lifetimes for sure. So they were evidently worried about friends and relatives who had passed before this occurred. Would those folks miss out on spending eternity with Jesus? Paul's answer: "The dead in Christ will arise first. Then we who are alive, who are left, will be caught up in the clouds together with them to meet the Lord in the air."

People today who advance this text as evidence of a coming rapture should consider this: Since two thousand years have passed, there apparently will be millions and millions of dead Christians who will come out of the ground and rise to the sky first; then the relatively few who are still alive will follow. Talk about night of the living dead. It's safe to say that is not how most people picture the rapture. But it's what the Bible describes. Furthermore, what have those deceased Christians been doing in the grave for hundreds of years — other than rolling over every now and then? When we die as Christians, we go to heaven, right? So aren't those saints already in heaven with Jesus? Evidently not, according to 1 Thessalonians 4.

Perhaps one might speculate that the souls of departed Christians are in heaven, and only their corpses remain in the grave awaiting their resurrected body when Jesus returns. Not only does the Bible never say anything like that anywhere, but in 1 Corinthians 15:35-57 Paul describes it differently. He writes: "For the trumpet will sound and the dead will be raised imperishable, and we [who are still alive] will be changed. For this perishable body must put on imperishability, and this mortal body must put on immortality." Yeah, I know this is confusing (like trying to divide 873 by 41 in your head), but it sounds here like we aren't immortal until we get our resurrected body, when Jesus returns. According to Paul, Christ has been raised, but nobody else has. Dead Christians are not raised until Jesus comes back, at which time they get their new body—which is a spiritual, immortal body—and finally defeat sin and death. For Paul, the resurrected body is crucial, but no one has received it because Christ has not yet returned. Are you still with me (the answer, by the way, is 21.29)? Therefore, when you die, apparently you do in fact hang out in the coffin until Jesus returns, which fits with 1 Thessalonians 4, but not with how most Christians imagine it will all go down—or up. I have no idea what happens if you are cremated.

These difficulties are essentially the result of Paul thinking that Christ's return was imminent. He had no idea we'd still be here a couple millennia later. It is worth reflecting for a moment on the fact that the man who wrote a good bit of the Bible was so mistaken about such a basic question. From the outside looking in, we should understand how silly it looks: Paul was wrong, and yet Christians—at least some of them—are still waiting. If this were not our Scripture, our tradition, wouldn't we chuckle at such naivety—not to mention the belief that millions of dead people will emerge from their tombs and float into the clouds.

Speaking of the clouds, now what about heaven? First Thessalonians 4 declares that when the saints meet the returning Christ in the sky, they "will be with the Lord forever" (4:17). But where that takes places is not clear. Most would assume heaven, but the text does not say so. In fact, when we search for any sort of description of heaven in the Bible, we are hard pressed to identify one. Earlier, we pointed out the difficulties in understanding the New Testament concept of hell. Heaven's no better — well the place is better, presumably, but figuring it out is no easier. The word "heaven(s)" appears frequently in the Old Testament, but there it refers to the skies, or the place where God and the angels dwell. It is not a place where people go when they die, as there is no belief in an afterlife in Hebrew thought. Even in the New Testament, heaven is not a destination where one goes at death. In fact, there is not one verse in the Bible which states that when a person expires, they go either to heaven or to hell. Simply not there.

Revelation 21 is where we get most of our ideas about heaven — no tears and streets of gold. But this passage is actually a description of the "new Jerusalem coming down out of heaven" since the first heaven and earth had passed away (21:1- 2). More importantly, this "new heaven" — yes, a second heaven — does not emerge until the very end of time; so the no-tears-streets-of-gold paradise does not exist yet, or at least no one occupies it. It's not where deceased saints go. According to the text, this "new heaven" is one city, here on earth, and it certainly seems to be a physical place — as opposed to a spiritual one — as its specific dimensions are given: turns out it's a giant cube. But Paul, however, says our resurrected bodies are not physical (1 Corinthians 15). So how then do our spiritual bodies walk on "streets of gold"? How can one even have a "spiritual body" — isn't that an oxymoron, like "round square" or "amicable divorce"?

The truth is that the Bible hardly has any discussion of heaven and the "rapture" — and what it does say is quite obscure. If anyone pretends otherwise, they are serving sugar and spice and everything nice (which might be what they serve in paradise, if that's the same thing as heaven).

RAW REFLECTIONS

As Christians we should have a basic grasp of the foundations of our beliefs, where they come from and how they developed. It's a long, complex history of which the Bible is only one part. The impression that we often receive from our clergy, however, is that there has always been one true, orthodox faith that has affirmed the doctrines outlined in the Bible from day one. But it is not that simple. That's the delightful version. The raw truth is much more complicated and harder to digest. So how might we do that?

First, the indispensable reflection: The Bible does not offer us clear, unambiguous answers to doctrinal questions. And think how easily it could have done that. Why not just lay it out manifestly and systematically for everyone to see? It could be a book of catechisms, answering all of our queries about everything from the mystery of the Trinity to whether or not we should baptize babies. But instead it offers us the opportunity to explore and engage, to think for ourselves, to love God with our minds. And that is what we must do.

The Bible works much like one of Jesus' parables: we ask a question and we get a story, not a solution. We want an answer, but instead we are given narratives and letters, poems and songs. When it comes to the big doctrinal issues, then, Scripture is something of a conversation partner whose thoughts are eclectic and who sometimes has nothing much to say. We must treat the Scripture with the same respect that we would show toward a good friend. We cannot make it say what we think it should say or what we've been taught to think it says. We cannot force it to fit with our own views. The Bible does not preach at us, dogmatically pushing a single agenda. It talks with us, openly and honestly. We then should respond in kind not only in our dealings with the Bible but also, and perhaps more imperatively, with each other.

In the face of the Bible's reticence and fogginess concerning many of our core creeds, it's appropriate — necessary, even — to admit our lack of understanding, to acknowledge the tentative nature of our beliefs. Such an attitude fosters a context for productive dialogue. It cultivates a sense of tolerance and respect not only for those within our Christian community who might think quite differently from us, but also for those outside of our faith tradition. If the Bible includes a wide range of diverse views — even on topics as fundamental as salvation — then why should we insist on only one correct one? If the Bible does not offer a single answer, then maybe there isn't one. If the Bible does not have much to say about a subject — like the nature of heaven and hell — then maybe we shouldn't either. If our Scripture does not contain clear answers to the big doctrinal questions, then why do we feel like we have to?

Rather, we must appreciate that many voices have contributed to the development of our doctrinal statements. Tradition is important. The views of Augustine, Origen, Clement, and Aquinas are tremendously valuable; they have shaped our beliefs in profound ways. Likewise, it's essential that Christians understand that the emergence of more recent theological views are just that: recent. They, like all creeds, have arisen in a specific social and cultural setting, which does not in any way delegitimize them, but it does put them in their proper historical context. For example, the belief that one becomes saved by "asking Jesus into your heart" and having a "personal relationship with Jesus" developed out of the Great Awakening in the United States in the 1800s. No Christian before then would have ever made such statements or articulated their experience in such terms. Christians who employ this language today should realize where it fits into the larger tradition: it hasn't been around from day one, or even day ten thousand. The same is true of numerous other elements. Christian language, beliefs, and practices change, which means that we would do well to hold doctrines tentatively. We are a part, after all, of a living, dynamic faith of which the Bible is one living, dynamic voice.

For the dispensable reflection, here are my own thoughts. Keep in mind how insignificant they are. For me, the nature of Scripture suggests that orthodoxy, right belief, isn't that important. Or at least it's not as important as orthopraxy, right action. I recall sitting in an undergraduate theology class listening to a lecture on the early church's arguments about how the divine and human nature cohered in Christ. It was riveting—if you were a true nerd. I just couldn't understand why, ultimately, it mattered. I say this, you say that; but what's the difference, really, at the end of the day. I remember raising my hand and asking what Scripture had to say. The answer was "very little." Well, I mused, the Bible gives us so much fodder for thought that maybe we should spend our time talking about the issues that we do find in Scripture (okay, I probably did not think those exact words, but that was the gist). That's why I decided to pursue a degree in biblical studies rather than theology or philosophy.

In other words, this course of the raw meal is not my favorite one. Yes, it's vital to ponder and debate these major creedal questions, but not to have schisms over them. Maybe, however, such schisms are an inevitable, if unfortunate, result of people engaging the Scripture and other voices in the tradition with their mind. The Bible's variety does in fact parallel and anticipate the multiplicity of the Christian tradition. I wish we could have diversity without division. To that end, I hold my doctrines loosely, knowing that I see through the glass dimly.

So what do I say specifically to some of the doctrinal subjects? Let me rip through some very brief responses, so as not to waste any of your time.

The fact that the Bible does not declare God to be the "omnis" is not surprising, given how it does depict God. Even if it did, though, I would see that as simply one more wonderful paradox for us to struggle with. The notion of the Trinity fits nicely with my sense that God is complex. God is big and in many ways beyond human comprehension. It also suggests that God is relational. The idea of three persons dynamically relating as one serves as a compelling model for our understanding of reality: it's all somehow interconnected, yet separate. Moreover, the concept of the Trinity says that God is one, yet God is manifested to us in multiple, different ways (Father, Son, Holy Spirit). We might extend and apply that principle beyond our faith tradition. God is revealed in various forms; thus God cannot be contained in one religion. There are not many paths to God; God takes many paths to us. The Trinity epitomizes how God relates to humanity. The three-ness of the Trinity points not literally to three, but to multiplicity. We, therefore, should be open to a variety of ways in which God might interact with humankind. (That wasn't so brief — I'll do better.)

God is beyond gender; thus we should try our best to refer to her/him/God accordingly.

I commented on my view of Jesus in the last course. In light of the heavier doctrinal questions surrounding his identity, I will just say this: I wish we had a DNA sample from Jesus.

The Holy Spirit is a symbol of God's working in us.

As for salvation, I deem it risky to ignore what Jesus says. I don't think he would appreciate it. I don't know where that leaves most of us. But . . .

It's difficult for me to conceive of a literal hell for a very simple and oft-articulated reason: God is love, and love doesn't torture people for rejecting them. Think of the person you hate the most, the person who has spit in your face countless times, and ask yourself if you would really condemn them to burn alive forever and ever and ever. Hell is real, just not a real place.

Likewise, Satan is real, just not a real person or being. He (It? She?) represents all that is evil and wicked in the world. Satan is everything that is opposed to God and good.

Concerning church and the sacraments, I think rituals and ceremonies are an important aspect of human existence and should be practiced in ways that are most meaningful to you. As long as it does not include actual cannibalism.

I would recommend giving away as much of your money as possible to those who need it most (!) and in ways that will foster independence for the recipient.

I do not know when the world as we know it will end, but I'd bet (literally, if I could) that nuclear war and/or climate change will have something to do with it. I do not know if there will be a second coming, but I doubt it will be a physical rapture. I do not know if, or what, or where heaven is.

I like the narrative, the characters, the plots, the laments, the hymns, the erotic love poetry (especially the erotic love poetry) that we do find in Scripture. It's hard for me to get into doctrine and philosophy. This is a weakness on my part. I tire of endless abstract debates about how Jesus could be fully God and fully human, about the nature of the Holy Spirit, or what heaven is like, or whether or not the wine (or Welches) is transformed into the blood of Jesus. So when it comes to this round of the meal, I tend to scrunch my face, lift my palms, and shrug my shoulders. But there are plenty of nerds — and I say that lovingly — for you to consult.

MORALITY

The fifth — but not quite final — course of our meal continues with many of the themes from the fourth one, namely, the Scripture's silence and ambiguity. But now we shift from doctrinal questions to moral, ethical, and social issues; that is, from belief to practice. If the Bible has relatively little to say about many Christian beliefs, one can imagine how little it has to offer about specific contemporary subjects, such as abortion, homosexuality, marriage, and the environment. What the Bible does not say is often as important as what it does say. The gaps are significant; they tell us something about Scripture's nature and purpose, its interests and goals — which, as it turns out, have little to do with the trying and practical questions we face today. That's a tough pill for many preachers to swallow.

In their effort to make the Bible meaningful and applicable to our lives — a laudable objective — church leaders address subjects and push agendas which the Bible does not. Based on the impression that some preachers give, one might assume, for example, that the Bible has a fair bit to say about premarital sex, family life, and money. But it doesn't. Now, this fact doesn't mean the Bible is irrelevant or that it has no role to play in current debates. It just means that we Christians need to understand on whose authority certain ideas are based. Again, it's not the Bible, nor is it even a long history of church tradition, as was the case with doctrinal issues. Rather, it's current Christian leaders. But they'd prefer that we not think of it that way.

The Bible's taciturnity allows preachers a great deal of latitude in the application of "biblical principles" to today's specific problems. But who determines which passages are relevant, what principle we are to derive from them, and which principle applies in which situation is all rather tricky, which is why there is no one single Christian view on, say, homosexuality or abortion. Different churches interpret the scant biblical data differently. This is to be expected (even embraced?). The problem emerges when people ignore the Scripture's silence and complexity, when they take their own positions and then quote the Bible as if it's plainly on their side. That's cooking the Good Book; that's not being forthright and truthful.

This course of the meal does not fill the biblical gaps; it only exposes them. It needs to be made clear from the outset that I am neither arguing one side of an issue or the other; nor am I suggesting that just because the Bible doesn't condemn a behavior indicates that it is morally and ethically appropriate, or that because it does not give express approval, it must be taboo. The Bible says nothing about pedophilia, for instance, but there are plenty of good reasons to judge it morally reprehensible. The Bible never tells wives to love their husbands, but that would seem to be a good idea – a really good idea. To be sure, we are confronted today with a variety of complex questions which require careful thought and reading and conversation, including a consideration of how the Bible might be brought to bear on the issue. Thus, we must know what the Bible does and does not say, so that we are not seduced into believing that our preacher's views, whatever they may be, are clearly substantiated by the Bible.

Is Homosexuality Wrong?

The Bible offers no easy answers – in some cases no answers at all – about a variety of issues related to human sexuality. Imagine if Titus 7:6 said, "Homosexuality, defined as deliberate and willing sexual contact between two adult men or between two adult women, regardless of the status of their relationship or emotional connection to one another, is an abomination before God." If it did, then there would be fewer books to write about the Bible and homosexuality. But it doesn't – there is no Titus 7:6. Frankly, there's hardly anything to consider at all.

The Old Testament condemns homosexuality. Twice and only male homosexuality. Leviticus 18:22 and 20:13 assert that a man should not lie with a man as with a woman. The latter verse proscribes death as the penalty. That's it for the Old Testament: 39 books, over 23,000 verses and two of them outlaw male homosexuality. There is nothing about a woman being with a woman, which is not surprising since it was written by men. Of course, to be consistent, if one cites these two verses as reasons to oppose homosexuality, then one would also need to oppose a man having sexual relations with his wife during her period, since that too is banned in the same passage (Leviticus 18:19). Both acts, along with others, cause the offender to be "cut off" from God's people (Leviticus 18:29). Apparently, God enjoys puns.

There are a few other Old Testament stories which can be mentioned. In Genesis 19, the men of Sodom surround Lot's house and demand that Lot's male guests — divine beings, it seems — be handed over so that they could have sex with them. Lot offers his two virgin daughters to the mob of men instead (always a benevolent gesture), but fortunately the guests are able to intervene and deter the attack. God then destroys Sodom. People have argued back and forth about whether or not this text pertains to God's disapproval of homosexuality. There is certainly a homosexual element to the story, followed by divine destruction of those men. The text, however, does not assert explicitly that Sodom was destroyed because of their homosexual intentions, only because of their wickedness. God had already decided to destroy Sodom — it's not a direct response to the attempted homosexual rape. God also destroys more than just Sodom; he burns Gomorrah and all the Plain as well (19:24-25). So it would be hard to argue that God is responding to and targeting only the homosexual behavior. In addition, we would do well to ask if same-sex gang rape, which is what we have in Sodom (or almost have), is in any way pertinent to a debate about the propriety of a mutually loving homosexual relationship.

Like the narrative about Sodom, the stories of David and Jonathan are often mentioned in this discussion. The biblical text, of course, does not say anything explicitly, but there are some rather suggestive elements. In 1 Samuel 18:1-4 we read, "The soul of Jonathan was bound to the soul of David, and Jonathan loved him as his own soul." David chooses not to return to his father's house, but remains with Jonathan. "Then Jonathan made a covenant with David because he loved him as his own soul." To seal the covenant, "Jonathan took off the robe he was wearing and gave it to David, along with his tunic, and even his bow, his sword, and his belt." Whether or not Jonathan is naked in this scene, two men who love each other, live together, and enter into a partnership signified by the exchanging of clothes could imply a sexual relationship. Moreover, in 1 Samuel 20:41, David and Jonathan wait to be alone and then they embrace, kiss, and cry together before parting ways. Later, after Jonathan has died, David mourns for him saying, "You were very dear to me; your love to me was wonderful, more wonderful than that of a woman" (2 Samuel 1:26). When my students read 1-2 Samuel, there are always a few of them who, totally unprompted, think it's quite obvious that they are lovers.

We can make of this relationship whatever we want—the text leaves plenty of room to go either way, if you will. A helpful experiment might be to ask ourselves: If the text made these sorts of statements about a man and a woman, would we assume that they were sexually intimate? Of course, even if we conclude that David and Jonathan were more than just friends, that does not necessarily mean that the text is endorsing their relationship, or that the stories have anything whatsoever to do with the question of homo-sexuality today.

Turning to the New Testament, there is nothing in the Gospels about homosexuality. Jesus does not mention it one time. Jesus was outspoken on a number of issues. But he has nothing to say about homosexuality. Interesting. Let's let that fact sink in for a moment.

Paul addresses homosexual behavior in Romans 1:26-27, a passage which has evoked copious commentary which we will not rehearse here. It reads: "Because of this, God gave them over to shameful lusts. Women exchanged natural intercourse for unnatural. In the same way, the men also abandoned natural relations with women and were consumed with passion for one another. Men committed shameful acts with other men, and received the due penalty for their error."

These two verses are a good example of ones that must be read in context, so we should be sure to take a minute to consider Romans 1:18-32. It's a peculiar section in which Paul vigorously denounces idolatrous religious worship and rituals. Its overall theme is the problems that arise when one does not properly acknowledge God (verses 21 and 28). Here are a couple of questions for our consideration regarding only verses 26-27:

What does it mean that "God gave them over"? The word "exchanged" is key in this chapter; what does Paul mean that women and men "exchanged natural intercourse for unnatural"? Are these formerly heterosexuals who engage in homosexual activity? Are these former believers who have turned away from the faith? Is Paul lambasting only "unnatural" as opposed to "natural" homosexual behavior? What does "consumed with passion" mean?

Is Paul talking about some orgiastic frenzy? Does Paul's description here seem to have any similarity to a situation in which two people are in a committed same-sex relationship? What is the "penalty for their error" — why not spell out the consequence clearly? Furthermore, Paul argues that idolatrous worship leads to unnatural intercourse as well as to every kind of wickedness, evil, covetousness, malice, envy, murder, strife, and deceit. Those who have unnatural intercourse are lumped together with those who are slanderers, gossips, God-haters, insolent, haughty, boastful, rebellious, foolish, faithless, heartless, and ruthless (verses 29-31). Why does Paul do this? Does that suggest that he is thinking of homosexuality in a way completely different from our cultural context?

It's a sticky passage. We indeed have a bit of work to do before we can make a judgment about what Paul means here. And then once we arrive at a (hopefully tentative) answer, we must ask ourselves if this passage is in any way germane to us today. By the way, whatever we conclude about homosexuality, we should be sure that our behaviors are not included in the long list in verses 29-31 — as those are just as reprehensible as "unnatural intercourse."

There are two other texts to consider, but things here are even more slippery. First Corinthians 6:9 and 1Timothy 1:10 use the very confusing word *arsenokoitai*. Paul appears to have coined this term — made it up — and it is thus difficult to know precisely what he had in mind. "Arsen" means "man" in Greek, so presumably the term cannot refer to both male and female homosexuality, even though most translations imply this by rendering it simply "homosexual behavior." The term may distinguish between passive and active participants in homosexual acts, which was a common way of reasoning in antiquity, but not so much today (I think). In both of these verses, the word appears alongside other familiar vices which prevent one from inheriting the kingdom of God: fornication, idolatry, thievery, greed, and drunkenness.

Again, we must contemplate how this context should shape our interpretation. We might ask conservative preaches why they take a strong stand against homosexuality—if that is what the verse is referring to—and ignore "greed" as an equally offensive action. Or we might ask more liberal pastors why they choose to focus on greed instead of the sexual offenses.

That's it for homosexuality and the New Testament. Nearly 8,000 verses, and four, at most, address homosexuality. If you are looking for clarity, you won't be very gay—as in happy.

CAN I DO THE DEED BEFORE I GET MARRIED?

Imagine if there were a verse in the Bible which addressed pre-marital sex by saying something like: "Sexual relations between two consenting adults in a committed relationship, even though not married, is acceptable." Unfortunately for all the Bible college couples, that verse is not there. And unfortunately for all the abstinence preachers, there is nothing which expressly forbids consensual premarital sex either. So in a world where we encourage young people not to get married until a decade after their sexual drives kick in, the church has to deal with this question. Wouldn't life be so much easier if we got married in our teens?

While a number of passages undeniably condemn adultery, there is no word used in the Bible to refer specifically to sexual relations prior to marriage. Several Old Testament laws deal with the topic, but we don't hear about them because they so obviously assume a different cultural context: the young woman was considered the property of her father and her virginity was of monetary value (which, as the father of a daughter, is not an altogether bad idea). Exodus 22:16-17, for instance, states that if a man has sex with a virgin, he is required to marry her. If the girl's father will not allow it, then the man must pay the father the bride price. Here the man and woman are not punished for having sex. The punishment is for the change in the woman's status: she is no longer a virgin and thus has lost her economic value to her father, so the man must pay the father what he took — the price of her virginity (that would make today's teenage boys think twice, wouldn't it). In Deuteronomy 22:28-29, incidentally, there is no option of paying the bride price. The man must marry the girl and never divorce her; it's the one-strike-and-your-in-law (and that would make the teenage girls think twice).

Deuteronomy 22:20-21 pertains to a woman who is found not to be a virgin when she marries. Her penalty is death — a verse I will share with my daughter. No such law exists for men who are not virgins when they marry — which I will not point out to my son. There are in fact no Old Testament laws governing the premarital sexuality of men. A man could do whatever he wanted as long as it did not violate a woman whose sexuality belonged to another man. There also are no laws regarding young women who are not engaged and not virgins. That is, if a woman's sexuality were not owned by a man — if she were not a virginal daughter or a wife — there were no restrictions placed on her. She too could evidently do as she pleased. Thus, interestingly, there are no Old Testament laws against prostitution, provided it was not associated with religious practices. At any rate, all of this has little relevancy for premarital sexual relations today.

The Old Testament does contain a book celebrating human sexuality, without any mention of marriage. The Song of Songs — or Song of Solomon — is a book of erotic love poetry replete with numerous sexual innuendos, including oral sex enjoyed by both the man and the woman (2:3 and 4:16 — if these are the first two verses you have looked up while reading this book, shame on you). The lovers in the Song of Songs do not appear to be married. They don't even live in the same house; rather they are separated and longing for a time and place to enjoy a passionate rendezvous. It would have been rather easy for the text to refer to them as husband and wife, but it doesn't. Yes, the male speaker refers to the girl as his "bride," but he also refers to her as his "sister" (e.g., 4:10). Both are simply terms of endearment. We should also remember that Solomon had 700 wives and 300 concubines (1 Kings 11:3), so if it's married sex, it's certainly not monogamous married sex.

The New Testament has no passages that explicitly address premarital sex. The word "fornication" is a translation of the Greek word *pornea*, which occurs in 32 verses (e.g., Matthew 5:32; Romans 1:29-31; 1 Corinthians 5:1; Galatians 5:19-20). Much has been written about this term and how best to translate it. It refers broadly to "sexual immorality," but just what that includes is not clear. Based on the social context of the early churches, it probably refers to adultery, prostitution, bestiality, incest, and sex between older men and boys.

Jesus, for example, uses the term *pornea* in Matthew 5:32 to refer to adultery—sex with someone other than your spouse: "Whoever divorces his wife, except for *pornea*, causes her to commit adultery." Similarly, it is evident that Paul included sex with prostitutes as *pornea*. These situations, however, are obviously different from premarital sexual relations in our culture. Jesus, as we saw earlier, taught that if a divorced person engaged in sexual intercourse with anyone—even if with a second spouse!—they are guilty of adultery. We can say without a doubt, then, that Jesus was adamantly against post-divorce sex, but he never spoke about premarital intercourse. By contrast, how many pastors have nothing to say about sex in re-marriage, but yet preach abstinence pre-marriage? That is not what Jesus did.

The Bible, in short, does not forbid consensual sexual relations between a male and female who have never been married, assuming one of them is not a prostitute. Some, no doubt, will argue that "premarital sex" is included as part of *pornea*, "sexual immorality." That could be. But that's what they say, not the Bible. People are free to include whatever they wish under the term *pornea*, even, say, masturbation.

Speaking of which, masturbation is not addressed anywhere in the Bible either. The Bible is written by men, so perhaps that has something to do with it not being condemned. Some people point to verses about keeping one's thoughts pure and not lusting as the "biblical principle" which suggests that masturbation is a sin. Actually, if we want to do some creative proof-texting, our best bet is: "Whatever your hand finds to do, do it with all your might." Seriously, though, there are a few texts that are commonly mentioned here.

In the story in Genesis 38 Onan "spills his seed" on the ground, and God kills him. Thus God, it is argued, hates masturbation. Onan's actions however have nothing to do with masturbation, which is apparent if you read the story. He is engaging in *coitus interruptus* — withdrawing, pulling out — so that his own children would not have to share the inheritance with their deceased uncle's offspring. God is angry with Onan, in other words, because he is not fulfilling his legal duties. There are a handful of laws in the Old Testament which declare a man "unclean" if he has an emission of semen, regardless if it's a result of intercourse with his wife (Leviticus 15:18), nocturnal emission (Deuteronomy 23:10), or for some other reason (Leviticus 15:16). That is, ejaculating by masturbation would have been treated the same as if it occurred by conjugal sex or a wet dream — completely natural. Likewise, Song of Songs 5:2-6 seems to allude to female masturbation as part of healthy human sexuality.

That's it. When it comes to masturbation, the Bible, we might say, turns a blind eye. So you are on your own.

LOVE AND MARRIAGE—DO THEY REALLY GO TOGETHER?

It is not uncommon for churches to hold marriage conferences or classes on parenting with titles like "Growing Kids God's Way" or "God's Design for Marriage," which claim to be based on biblical principles. To be sure, there are wonderful passages of Scripture which call Christians to love, honor, and serve others. Such texts might indeed provide the base for healthy marriages and family relationships. But the problem is that the Bible does contain material that directly addresses family related issues. But they are too raw for our palates.

First of all, we should remind ourselves of the Old Testament metaphor which depicts God as the husband and the people of Israel as his wife, which we considered earlier. Let's be honest: Could there be a more obvious and appropriate place to begin a book or seminar about how to be a "Godly husband" than to look at how God himself plays that role? These passages, of course, are never mentioned, and for good reason: God is a jealous, violent, abusive, and manipulative husband. He is not a model that any decent human being would emulate. Biblical principle number one for husbands: Don't be like God.

As for God's role as a parent, there are a variety of Old Testament passages which employ the parent-child metaphor to describe the relationship between God and Israel. While some of them show God the father to be long-suffering and compassionate (Hosea 11), there are others which are downright chilling. In Deuteronomy 32 God tells how he provided for his children (verses 7-15) only to be rejected by them. In response to their recalcitrance, God "spurned his sons and daughters," saying: "I will hide my face from them; then we will see what will happen to them; for they are a perverse generation. . . . I will heap disasters on them and shoot my arrows against them. I will send wasting famine against them, burning pestilence, and deadly plague. I will send against them the fangs of wild beasts, the venom of vipers that crawl in the dust. In the street the sword will make them childless, in their homes terror will reign. Young men and women will perish, infants and those with gray hair. I had planned to scatter them and erase their name from the face of the earth; but I feared the taunt of the enemy, for their adversaries might misunderstand and say, 'We have triumphed; the Lord has not done all this'" (Deuteronomy 32:19-27).

We must deal with this metaphor, unfiltered: Here God is a father with serious psychological problems. Read that last verse again. God intends to utterly destroy his children, but he doesn't only because he fears he won't get the credit! The rest of Deuteronomy 32 continues in the same dark vein as God vaunts his power over both Israel and its enemies: "There is no God beside me. I kill and make alive; I wound and I heal; and no one can deliver from my hand" (verse 39). This parent-child relationship is sad and deeply broken; it's marked by constant tension, strife, and pain (e.g., see also Judges 10). Biblical principle number two: Don't parent God's way.

The Old Testament also contains laws which deal explicitly with the family unit, but they too offer little worthwhile fodder. Men were permitted to have multiple wives; a man could divorce his wife simply because she did not please him (Deuteronomy 24:1); fathers were allowed to sell their daughters into slavery (Exodus 21:7); families owned slaves (Deuteronomy 21:18-21; Exodus 21:2); children born to slaves were the property of the master (Exodus 21:2-4); and disobedient children were to be killed (Exodus 21:15). True, it's the Old Testament, so what do we expect. But still, we should consider the implications of laughing off these passages when promoting "good, biblical family values."

If the Old Testament is of no help, what about the New Testament's specific advice concerning marriage and the family? It's not much better. First, in 1 Corinthians 7 Paul recommends that people not get married: "To the unmarried and the widows I say that it is well for them to remain unmarried as I am. But if they cannot control themselves, they should marry. For it is better to marry than to burn with passion (7:8-9). The "unmarried" probably refers to widowers—the word is masculine. They were not to remarry unless they could not control their sexual urges. Paul gives the same advice to single people—"virgins"—in verses 25-28: "In view of the present crisis, it is well for you to remain as you are. Are you bound to a wife? Do not seek to be free. Are you free from a wife, do not seek a wife." Paul further explains that even if someone is already engaged, it's best to hold off getting married. However, if you cannot control your bodily desires, then it's appropriate to get hitched, even though that's not as good as remaining unattached (verses 36-38). According to Paul, then, the primary reason to get married is for fleshly gratification, which is quite unlike what any preacher or Christian counselor will say today—hopefully. Paul, incidentally, being a single man, does not recognize that marriage and sex ought not to be equated—at least after a while.

Paul's advice is based on his firm conviction that Christ was returning soon—"the present crisis" in verse 26 refers to the tribulations that were expected to occur just prior to the end. He also says, "The appointed time has grown short: from now on, let even those who have wives be as though they had none" (verse 29). Now there's a verse we aren't likely to hear in a wedding ceremony—though it would serve as a wonderful proof-text for husbands when they, say, forget their anniversary. Given Paul's mistaken belief, and the fact that we are still here two thousand years later, preachers simply shrug off his words as relevant only to the original audience.

Another aspect of Paul's teaching, however, is much harder to dismiss. Paul argued that married life was stressful and posed a distraction from serving God. "Those who marry will experience distress in this life, and I would spare you that" (verse 28). So, turns out, Paul does know quite a bit about married life. He continues, "I want you to be free from anxieties. The unmarried man is anxious about the affairs of the Lord; but the married man is anxious about the affairs of the world, how to please his wife, and his interests are divided" (verses 32-34). The same thing goes for married women (verses 34-35). This advice is seemingly not limited to a certain time and place. It has, in fact, had a large impact on the Catholic Church requiring celibacy of its priests (which was the first of many reasons I did not become a monk). As Paul very clearly says: If you are married, your "interests are divided" between the affairs of family life and the affairs of God — and then sometimes there are just affairs. Thus, don't get married. In light of God's rocky and embattled relationship with his wife Israel perhaps such advice is sensible and consistent.

Here, then, is clear "biblical teaching" about marriage and the family. It's plain and simple. There are no principles to apply; there is no guess work involved. It's straightforward and it's from the New Testament, not the Old. What more do we want?

Like the tough sayings of Jesus, this is one of those passages that preachers explain away with phrases like, "The main idea here is . . ." or "If we first consider the situation in Corinth at the time . . ." or "What Paul is really saying . . . " or "When we look at other passages . . ." Such statements are smooth interpretive moves to dilute the plain meaning of the text. Biblical principle number three: Don't get married.

When the New Testament does come around to discussing married life, it only gets more unpleasant. Most of us are probably unfamiliar with the aforementioned 1 Corinthians 7 — as pastors ignore it — but the texts about "wives submit to your husbands" have garnered more attention (though I am not sure why). There are several passages which outline the codes of conduct for Christian households, including Ephesians 5:21-6:9 and Colossians 3:18-4:1, both of which instruct, "Wives, submit to your husbands as unto the Lord, for the husband is the head of the wife just as Christ is the head of the church." And it gets tougher: "Just as the church is subject to Christ, so also wives ought to be, in everything, subject to their husbands." In everything. That's every thing. Fist bump for the macho men.

Yes, husbands are told to love their wives (5:33). But the simple fact is that if these were not the Bible's words, but those of a preacher, we'd probably be aghast and offended, and said preacher would not be around long. That's because most people today understand the marriage relationship rather differently. We would say that both the husband and the wife should love and respect each other. Unfortunately that is not the way Scripture puts it. Nowhere in the Bible, astonishingly, are wives commanded to love their husbands (something women may want to note). What would we say if this type of hierarchical language concerning husbands and wives appeared in the sacred text of another religious tradition?

Now let's finally get to the tough stuff, 1 Peter 2:18-3:7 — which gets my vote for the rawest in the entire New Testament. Check out the whole thing for yourself. Here's what it says in summary: Slaves obey your masters and submit to them, no matter how harshly they treat you. Endure the pain and suffering. Remember that when Jesus was abused, he did not fight back, but accepted it passively and trusted God. So follow the example of Christ's suffering. Wives, in the same way, accept the authority of your husbands, so that you might win them over, if they are unbelievers. Focus on your inward beauty like the women of times past who accepted their husband's authority. Remember Sarah who obeyed Abraham and called him Lord. Be like her. And husbands, be considerate of your wives, honoring them as the weaker sex.

This is not some obscure text from the Old Testament law. This is the New Testament. Not only are wives placed in a subordinate position in the household, but Peter exhorts them to submit to their husbands just as a slave submits to a cruel master. Wives should accept their husband's abuse just as Christ suffered. We must pause and picture what Peter is asserting here. Imagine a bloodied and bruised wife who quietly accepts her fate in an effort to be Christ-like. It's a painful image, I know. But it's what our Scripture says.

In sum, Christian books, marriage conferences, and parenting seminars aside, there is nothing whatsoever in the Bible about marrying for love, how to have romance in marriage, what men or women want, how to handle your rebellious teenager, or how to kill your teenager. Furthermore, if people gave actual "biblical" advice concerning the family, they'd recommend that singles never get married, that divorced and widowed people remain unattached, and that wives, as the weaker gender, are to be submissive in everything, including suffering under their abusive husbands in order to follow Christ's example. That's too raw. So instead we get the chargrilled version, which is typically the exact same advice given by any decent "secular" marriage or parenting book. But it sells better if it has "God" or "Bible" in the title.

WHEN DOES LIFE BEGIN?

I hate to keep saying the same thing, but consider how easily the Bible could have settled the abortion question. Somewhere it could have said, "Life begins at birth; the unborn fetus does not have the rights of a human person" or it could say, "Life begins at conception; therefore aborting a fetus is murder." Of course it does not make either of these statements. The fact is that the Bible says nothing about abortion. Nothing. Thus, once more, people must hunt for verses that appear to have some relevancy. Even then, there isn't much.

First, the command not to murder does not qualify as an argument against abortion. It begs the question: Is the fetus the same as a full term human person? The Bible provides no answer. Some can quote Genesis 2:7 to argue that life begins when there is breath, which does not occur until birth: "God breathed into his nostrils the breath of life and man become a living being." However, the context of this verse—God creating the first people— renders it highly suspect as germane to a debate about the status of a human fetus.

Others will cite Psalm 139:13-16 in support of the view that life begins at conception: "You knit me together in my mother's womb . . . Your eyes beheld my unformed substance." As we discussed in the previous course, it is quite problematic to proof-text from the Psalms because they make so many different claims about God—that he is absent, cruel, harsh, powerful, wonderful, and so on. Psalm

139 is the perspective of one human writer — not God — who is declaring that God knew him personally in the womb. He is not making a claim about the status of all fetuses, nor are the handful of other isolated verses which are similar to Psalm 139 (Job 31:15; Isaiah 49:1; Psalm 22:9-10; Luke 1:15; and Galatians 1:15).

Furthermore, Psalm 139 is metaphoric language, as is clear from verse 15 which says, "When I was being made in secret, intricately woven in the depths of the earth." The psalmist was not formed inside the earth; it's poetry so we understand what the writer means. But, as metaphoric poetry, it's difficult to take it as a passage that belongs in a discussion about abortion. Likewise, Jeremiah 1:5, which reads, "Before I formed you in the womb I knew you," would mean that life begins even before conception, which doesn't make much sense. Again, the poetic theology of the verse is evident — Jeremiah was born to be a prophet of God. But it has little to do with when life begins.

Job 3 is an interesting chapter because it discusses the moment of Job's conception. This passage, however, is hardly ever mentioned, especially by those who oppose abortion. In this deeply depressing text Job curses the day of his birth and the night of his conception: "Why did I not die at birth, come forth from the womb and expire? . . . Or why was I not buried like a stillborn child, like an infant that never sees the light of day?" (verses 11, 16). Life began in the womb, but Job wishes it had ended there (see also Job 10:18-19). It's not a particularly pro-life text. Neither is Ecclesiastes 6:3-6 which says that it's better to be aborted than to go through life unable to enjoy it (see also Ecclesiastes 4:1-3). Some, then, have suggested that perhaps these passages support the notion of terminating a pregnancy when a low quality of life seems inevitable. But that too is quite a stretch.

Leviticus 27:1-6 places monetary values on human beings. In verse 6, no value is placed on a child until they are one month old, implying that they did not have full human status until that point. Similarly, in Numbers 3:15, God commands the Israelites to take a census, but they were to count only those male children who were at least one month old. In light of the high rate of infant mortality in antiquity, was a newborn not considered a person until they reached that age?

One final text has possible significance here. Exodus 21:22-25 deals with a pregnant woman who is injured in a fight and as a result the baby "comes out." Many commentators, though not all, assert that "came out" refers to miscarriage—the baby is stillborn, or maybe is born and then dies. In the ancient world, it would have been nearly impossible to keep a premature baby alive—it can barely be done today with modern medicine. So when a woman, the reasoning goes, is injured and the baby "comes out," the perpetrator has effectively killed the baby, but not the woman. If this is the case, then the law places a much higher value on the life of the mother than on the fetus: If the woman is killed in the fight, it's considered murder, so the offender must also be killed. But if only the fetus dies, it's not deemed murder; so only a fine is paid.

Regardless of how one interprets these passages, Christians can make the claim that they are inconsequential since they are from the Old Testament. There is nothing in the New Testament that could reasonably be brought to bear on the subject of abortion.

HOW MUCH DEBT SHOULD I CARRY?

When it comes to money, preachers have a wide range of options from which to draw, including your bank account. So unlike our other discussions in this course, we won't be able to consider many of the texts that might be cited. Most of them, however, have little practical application for our contemporary world. But it's a preacher's job to make Scripture meaningful, so they quote selectively as they please. For some, it's a message of wealth and prosperity built on verses like Deuteronomy 8:18, "But you shall remember the Lord your God, for it is he who is giving you power to make wealth" or John 10:10 where Jesus says, "I am come that they might have life, and that they might have it more abundantly." Thus, God wants you to be rich.

Other ministers find such a message to be an appalling abuse of the Bible. They prefer the texts which devalue money and material possession. So they might choose 1 Timothy 6:7-10, "For we brought nothing into this world, and it is certain we can carry nothing out . . . But those who desire to be rich fall into temptation and a snare." Or Matthew 6:19-20, "But lay not up for yourselves treasures on the earth, where moth and rust corrupts, and where thieves break through and steal. But lay up for yourselves treasures in heaven."

Regardless of which text one might prefer, it is evident that none of them yield specific advice about how to handle your personal finances — how much to save, where to invest, or how to deal with debt. Still, preachers and Christian financial advisors use terms like "biblical financial principles," which are nothing more than strained attempts to make the Bible applicable to every area of our lives. As with marriage and family life, "biblical teaching" about money and personal finance amounts to nothing more than common sense ideas. By the way, isn't there something patently wrong with selling a Christian, "Bible based" financial program to help you get out of debt—and of course they accept credit cards.

In an earlier course we discussed several passages in which Jesus addressed money, so we will not repeat that here, other than to say that Jesus was not a big fan of wealth. Instead, let's mention one New Testament passage that speaks directly to a specific and relevant financial question: Debt. Thus we might expect to find it named frequently in discussions about money and the Bible. But we don't.

Romans 13:8 reads, "Owe no one anything, except to love one another." How much clearer can it be? Don't go into debt. It's pertinent, it's practical, and its' great advice. But, alas, that's a tough message to swallow in the culture in which we live, so it's conveniently overlooked—or overcooked. If it is addressed, we are sure to hear explanations like, "It means we should not go into *excessive* debt, or not let debt *control* us" or "The principle here is that we should *try to* live debt free, but it's fine if you need to borrow money, as long as you can pay it back." Anything to avoid the plain meaning.

Imagine if Romans 13:8 had said, "It's good and wise to use credit to purchase things you cannot afford at the moment." If it read that way, would preachers try to circumvent the evident meaning by saying, "Well, the idea here is that we should only borrow as little as possible and pay it back as soon as we can" or "What Paul really means is that using credit is bad, but God will tolerate it in unique circumstances, such as the purchase of a home." No, of course not. Preachers would be all over that verse like a lender on a loan application with a 790 credit score. Everyone would know Romans 13:8. But as it is, the biblical text is too raw for our sensitive palates—and indebted pocketbooks.

The Bible and money is a large topic, but we should be aware that preachers have a vested interest—pun intended—on how it is presented. The Bible is not a guide to practical financial matters. If we look hard enough and shine just the right light on it, we can find biblical texts to support just about any view on money matters, including that money does not matter at all.

SHOULD I DIET AND EXERCISE?

The same is true for physical health. The Bible is not a book that has anything to do with diet, nutrition, and fitness. The Bible has no interest whatsoever in spelling out how we should eat or in advocating some sort of exercise program. Yet, the Bible is linked with these various arenas of life by citing isolated verses. And surely by now we know the problem with that.

If we want the Bible to advocate a vegetarian diet, we quote Genesis 1:29 where God says, "See, I have given you every plant yielding seed that is on the face of all the earth, and every tree with seed in its fruit; you shall have them for food." If we like a good steak, we point to Genesis 9:3 where God says, "Every moving thing that lives shall be for food for you." If we think a Mediterranean diet is the way to go, we can point to the fact, as people have done, that Jesus fed the multitudes with bread and fish, not burgers and fries; thus Jesus recommends a diet of grain and sea life.

Likewise, if we enjoy our "adult beverages," we've got several passages at our disposal, such as Proverbs 31:6-7 and 1 Timothy 5:23 which extol the virtues of imbibing. And if we think the devil is in the bottle, there's Proverbs 23:29-35 and Ephesians 5:18 which warn of the dangers of drinking. Different texts, different answers. Thus, Christians can point to whichever one they want, which is why we have Baptists and Episcopalians.

By selectively quoting from virtually any big book, one can find texts to support whatever program one desires. We, for instance, could come up with The Shakespearean Diet or Twain-Based Nutrition. Frankly, here's how it works: Modern research outlines healthy eating practices and then people search the Bible looking for verses that might be in line with that. It's a way to promote the lucrative diet and health industry to a Christian audience. The Bible, however, has nothing to do with your physical well-being, at least not any more so than *Romeo and Juliet* or *Huckleberry Finn*.

SHOULD I BE CONCERNED ABOUT GLOBAL WARMING?

The Bible was written several thousand years ago before ecological concerns arose. Reading the Bible looking for instructions about how to treat the environment is like using it as a manual to your laptop. To be sure, in a book as large and diverse as the Bible, there will be passages which refer to the earth, plants, and animals, which means that preachers are able to use those verses to promote whatever view they wish.

To illustrate, let's listen to this short hypothetical conversation between a preacher who is a global warming skeptic (GWS) and a go-green pastor (GGP):

GWS: God made the earth's natural resources for us to use however we want. In Genesis 1:28 God says to the humans he has created, "Fill the earth and subdue it; and have dominion over the fish of the sea and over the birds of the air and over every living thing that moves on the earth." This is about as close to an environmental ethic as we find in the Bible. And it's obvious the world is made to de dominated by people—note the words "subdue" and "have dominion." Yes, a number of Christian scholars have made heroic efforts to reinterpret this text to mean that God intends for humans to have stewardship over the earth, instead of utter mastery and control. But this is a skewed left wing idea. God could have said, "Have compassion on the earth, all its plants and animals and natural resources." But it doesn't; so you environmentally conscious preachers are forced to explain "what the text really means" or ignore it. Likewise, God says to Noah after the flood: "The fear and dread of you shall rest on every animal of the earth, and on every bird of the air, on everything that creeps on the ground, and on all fish of the sea; into your hand they are delivered" (Genesis 9:2). See, in honor of this verse, here's my NRA membership card.

GGP: Yes, but what about Genesis 2:15: "Then the Lord God took the man and put him in the Garden of Eden to tend and keep it." Here we are enjoined to take care of the world, not subdue and have dominion over it. Note also that the Old Testament features laws that prescribe benevolent treatment of land and animals. Fruit-bearing trees were not to be cut down in siege warfare (Deuteronomy 20:19); fields and vineyards were to lie fallow every seven years (Leviticus 25:3-5); distressed animals were to be helped (Deuteronomy 22:1-4); and beasts of burden allowed to rest on the Sabbath (Exodus 20:10). These texts are evidence that God was way ahead of modern environmentalists. God has been preaching care for the natural world long before it was fashionable. Furthermore, the book of Psalms offers many praises for the beauty of creation (e.g., Psalm 104). Thus, I drive a hybrid and we recycle.

GWS: This is an utterly absurd argument—not to mention purchasing an electric car. You mean to tell me that God instructed the Israelites to take care of plants and animals, but he permitted them to beat their slaves, with no penalty (Exodus 21:20-21)? God was concerned about the environment, but did not care about a girl who got raped in a city (Deuteronomy 22:23-24)? Look, God himself destroys the whole world with a flood, and his express intention was to wipe out the animals (Genesis 6:7; 7:21-23). Likewise, when God rained fire and brimstone on Sodom and Gomorrah, he incinerated not only the cities, but also the plants around them as Genesis 19:25 makes clear. Oh, and then there's the book of Revelation where God destroys the whole world again. God obviously does not care about the environment—or if he does, he has an unusual way of showing it.

GGP: Ah, but you are misconstruing these texts. The point is that the violence and sin of humankind adversely affected the natural world, so God destroys them both. The life of humans and plants and animals is inextricably bound; therefore we should take care of them.

In short, the Bible does not offer much help for the environmental issues we confront—it does not prohibit or condone factory farming, the protection of endangered species, or the use of animals in experiments. People decide what they think about these questions, and then they go to the Bible and look for texts that could possibly bolster their position. But, again, Bible-based environmental ethics is about as meaningful as a Shakespearean ecology.

RAW REFLECTIONS

As Christians, the Bible should be included in our conversations about current issues. But we must face the fact that it provides no easy answers. It's not a straightforward guide to navigate the complex moral and ethical landscape we inhabit. We should be very suspicious of preachers who do not recognize this basic truth. The Bible must be handled with care and sensitivity; its voice must be heeded with reason and discernment. In order to do this, we must first acknowledge the Bible's lack of clarity. Then we can begin carefully, tentatively to examine and appropriate biblical perspectives as they relate to contemporary challenges, knowing that, in light of the reticence and diversity of Scripture, it will be a hazardous task and solutions will remain uncertain and consensus among believers will hardly, if ever, emerge. The Bible does not have all the answers. There is no need to act like we do.

As good orators and teachers know, there is tremendous power in silence. It gives people room to think; it creates space for reflection and conversation. Our Scripture understands this. Its quietness draw us in, inviting us to form our own ideas in consultation with others — other people, other books, other arenas of life that have something to contribute. There is power in the sense of community that develops through the process of conversation. "Process" and "communication" are key ideas: it takes time and it takes community to work through the difficult choices we face. Christians, then, should engage in lively debates about these issues, without allowing disagreements to cause fragmentation and isolation. Scripture's silence has opened a valuable space. We should use it wisely — as loving, open, honest people of faith.

We are not loving, open, and honest when we cherry-pick certain verses to support our own personal agendas. We shouldn't make the Bible say what we want it to say; we shouldn't put words in its mouth. And we should not let our preachers do it either. There is nothing wrong with being passionate about an issue; but we cannot fool ourselves into thinking that the Bible is obviously on our side. It's not.

Keep in mind that it was not too long ago that well-meaning Christians pointed to the Bible to support the institution of slavery. These were not bad people who purposely manipulated Scripture for their own ends. Instead their beliefs and practices were part of a particular cultural and religious context very different from our own. Cases such as this, and many others throughout the history of our faith, remind us that we should be cautious in our thinking about the controversial issues of our day. We, after all, could turn out to be just as wrong as the Christians who opposed abolition.

Wouldn't it be refreshing if preachers, like Paul who admitted when he was giving only his own opinion (1 Corinthians 7:25), said things such as, "I personally think abortion is wrong and that we should take care of the environment, but the Bible is unclear on these topics, so let me give the best case for my position based on my own thinking and reading and studying of a number of books, including the Bible." Or imagine a pastor going a step further and declaring, "I know that the Scripture teaches in several passages that the wife is to submit to her husband, but I respectfully think that is flat out wrong and here's why . . ." Isn't that type of candor much better than forcing the text to fit one's own personal platform, or ignoring the biblical perspective altogether. Don't we prefer preachers who handle Scripture with the same dignity and respect that we would show to a good friend with whom we do not always agree?

But if churches serve it to us unfiltered and unprocessed like this, things become more complicated. It's much safer and succulent to believe that there are clear-cut answers to the moral and ethical issues we confront. Quick and easy answers sell; so that is what we get. But the Bible does not pander to such adolescent desires. Rather, it teaches us that a life of mature, authentic faith is a lot messier.

For the dispensable conclusion, I am reluctant even to offer my own perspectives. But these are huge questions, and they are practical, so I cannot say, as I did with the doctrinal issues, that our answers have little significance for how we live our lives. Each topic addressed in this course is worthy of careful, reasoned conversation, so do not take my ridiculously concise remarks as an indication of the level of complexity involved. Take them as an indication of their (lack of) significance in the overall debate — and the fact that we have limited space. So here we go:

Our sexuality is a wonderful and powerful aspect of our humanity and it should be treated with utmost care and concern. As long as one understands this and makes thoughtful and responsible decisions regarding their sexuality, then we should be willing to accept a variety of choices. If God cared a lot about who had sex with whom, or when the sex was had, he could have said so clearly in the Bible. Still, I would say that we probably shouldn't have sex with animals.

Marry with caution, grave caution. Husbands and wives should love and respect each other. Parents should love their children, part of which they demonstrate through committed and consistent discipline. Children should be respected, but also obedient. We should not have slaves.

Christians should save more money and spend less. We should invest wisely with the intent of taking care of our children and giving to those in need, not amassing a nest egg for retirement. We should not live in excessively large houses.

We should eat plenty of fruits and vegetables, monitor diligently our consumption of alcohol, sugar, and red meat, and exercise regularly. We should not binge drink.

We should do our best to take care of the world that God has given us. I wish I was smart enough to understand the scientific debates on climate change, but it seems intuitively correct to me that within the last century, human activity has changed the environment in unnatural and unhealthy ways. To what extent and what we should do about it? That's hard to say. We should not litter.

Abortion is a more trying subject—hence let me offer a few more thoughts. Life is sacred and should be treated as such, but when exactly it begins is much trickier. Does a zygote have a soul? The most directly relevant biblical texts do not, in my honest interpretation, value the fetus (or even newborns) on par with adult humans. But I also recognize that I value human life much more than said passages. Let me underscore that I make a sincere effort to listen to what Scripture says, but conclude that it is not particularly meaningful for us today on this particular topic. So I must do more thinking and reading to develop my perspective. That includes considering what science can tell us.

Of the many insights that modern technology offers and which could be discussed here, I mention only two that are particularly striking to me personally. On the one hand, I am truly amazed at how quickly the fetus develops. It's practically a human by the end of the first trimester. This leads me to think that we should consider the unborn fetus the same as a fully-birthed human. On the other hand, the scientific data tells us that a large percentage of fertilized eggs never implant in the uterus. That means that if life begins at conception, most "people" are naturally aborted. This information makes me think that life does not begin at conception; and if it does not begin at that point, then who is to say when it begins. Would birth be the next best logical answer? (By the way, if life begins at conception and if "babies go to heaven," then heaven will be populated almost exclusively with people who lived only a day or two. That is counterintuitive to me.) In short, I am really not sure what to think.

It's absurd to reduce the abortion question to a paragraph. But it's not absurd to say that it's a tough question. And it certainly is not absurd — requisite even — to acknowledge that there is no biblical answer. Which is the case for many of the demanding moral issues of our time.

May we all strive together in peace and love toward knowledge and truth.

COURSE 6

OTHER MORSELS

There's nothing common and predictable about the unedited Bible, so why serve it up in the standard five courses? How about a sixth one with more raw goodness for our spiritual vitality.

Here we present some important facts about the Bible and our religious tradition. All of this is common material that preachers study in an introductory Bible class in college or seminary. But somehow it never finds its way into the church. It is true that textual criticism, canonization, hermeneutics, and archeology are not particularly good fodder for inspiring sermons. Nevertheless, this is very accessible data—despite the fancy, academic jargon—that Christians should have the opportunity to chew on. But few do. And preachers are content to keep it that way, since the more we know the more questions will arise. Those questions can be difficult to answer and their implications far reaching. But ignoring the facts won't make them go away.

So let's gather around God's banqueting table for one more round.

BETTER LATE THAN NEVER?

Christianity had a specific starting point in human history. And it was not that long ago. There are thousands of years of recorded history before our religion shows up on this planet. That's kind of important.

Christianity, like Judaism and Islam, is a historical religion. Its central beliefs are based on characters and events, unlike, say, Buddhism and Hinduism, which are more akin to philosophies and are not grounded on specific moments of the past. According to the stories in Genesis, God established a covenant with Abraham and promised to make his descendants into a great nation. If we trace the biblical chronology (always an enthralling exercise), we find that Abraham would have lived about 1600-2000 years before Jesus. Prior to Abraham there was no Israelite religion. Thus, according to the Bible itself, God first revealed himself to Abraham no more than two millennia before Jesus.

We must stop and ponder how late that is. Archaeological findings reveal the nature of human civilizations ten, twenty, thirty thousand years ago. But never mind all that. Writing developed in China, Egypt, and Mesopotamia between 3,000 and 4,000 B.C. That means we have written records of those cultures for more than a millennium before

Abraham shows up on the timeline of human history. We can read about the rise and fall of numerous cultures long before God appeared to Abraham. It's critical to acknowledge the simple fact that the "Father" of our faith is a relative late-comer. Millions of people lived and laughed and loved and developed ideas about god (God?) — and wrote about it all — prior to the origins of our religion. Countless people could say, "Before Abraham was, I am" (John 8:58). Christians tend to assume — incorrectly — that our religion has been around forever. It hasn't.

I know what you are wondering: What about Genesis 1-11 — how does that fit in? The narratives and genealogies in the first chapters of the Bible are penned by the ancient Israelites. Even if Moses wrote Genesis, he did so no more than 1,200 years before Jesus, which would be thousands of years after the events in Genesis 1-11 occurred. The opening chapters of the Bible are not an eyewitness account, as everybody knows. Furthermore, we cannot take the genealogical names and numbers in Genesis 1-11 as literal and accurate; it just doesn't work. First off, it says that people lived to be 900 years old (imagine the problems with health care and social security). But, more importantly, one single family line, beginning with Adam a few thousand years before Abraham, does not in any way account for the known vast diversity of humanity. It is evident from extensive and conclusive written and archeological records that countless people were living all over the globe many, many moons before Abraham. Genesis 1-11 can in no way be harmonized with this fact — because the writer(s) of Genesis had no concept that the Americas, China, or Papa New Guinea existed. If we read the genealogies in Genesis 1-11 literally, we essentially have to deny everything that is written in history and anthropology books concerning the ancient world. That is not loving God with our minds.

This, of course, has only to do with the establishment of Jewish religion. Christianity started a mere two thousand years ago. That's not even ancient history. We may tend to think of it as way-back-when; but in terms of the big picture, it was rather recent. Of all the major world religions, only Islam developed later.

So what does this mean? Quite a bit, it would seem. For one thing, we cannot declare that our religion is superior because it has stood the test of time. More crucially, though, this broader historical perspective raises a number of theological questions. If our God is the creator, why wait so long to reveal himself to Abraham? And why then wait another two thousand years to send Jesus—and why to the back woods of Palestine, if it were a message meant for everyone? If God loves equally everyone who has ever lived, why not reveal himself until so many of them are dead and gone? How could people who lived prior to Abraham—never mind before Jesus—have known about God? Is it sensible, then, to argue that Christianity is the one and only true way to know God? If so, then what about the millions of people who lived, say, in the Americas, thousands of years prior to Abraham?

In short, situating Christianity in the context of the history of the world serves to put us in our place, so to speak.

WHOSE CANON IS BIGGER?

No one person sat down and wrote the Bible. It is a collection of books written by many different people over a long period of time in a variety of places, as we noted back in our first course. So how exactly did these particular books end up in the Bible, as opposed to other ancient Israelite and Christian writings? When did this occur? And who was involved in making these crucial decisions? In stilted academic terms, we are asking about the formation of the canon—the list of sacred books that make up the Bible. "Canon," by the way, is not to be confused with "cannon," the large mounted cylindrical weapon that has to do with balls and shooting.

The answers to these questions concerning canonization are complex, but they are probably not as central as the questions themselves. Indeed, it is vital to recognize that the formation of the Bible took place over a long period of time; God did not drop it from heaven in the form that we know today. Rather, people argued about which books should be included and which ones omitted.

The super-abbreviated (you're welcome) version is this: The Jewish community in Palestine appears to have sanctioned the books that now make up the Hebrew Bible, that is, the Christian Old Testament, before the time of Jesus. There were many Jews, however, living outside of Palestine who had their own beliefs about which writings should be included. For instance, the Greek-speaking Jews living in the city of Alexandria in Egypt had a significantly larger canon—meaning more books in the Bible. Those are essentially the books of the Apocrypha, as the Protestant tradition calls them, or the Deuterocanonical works as they are denoted in Catholicism. More on that in a minute (try to curb your enthusiasm—I know the concept "deuterocanonical" can be exciting). Even the Jews in Palestine had discussions about the propriety of including certain texts, such as Esther, Ecclesiastes, and the Song of Songs. Ultimately, though, the Jews gave formal recognition to the list of books that we know as the Old Testament.

As for the New Testament, it is clear that for the first three or four centuries after Jesus different churches throughout the Roman Empire had their own list of sacred books. Most churches used some sort of collection of Paul's letters, and one or more of the four Gospels; but that is where the similarities ended. Many groups rejected the books of Revelation (probably not a bad idea), 2 Peter, and James and accepted a number of works that are completely unfamiliar to us, such as the Apocalypse of Peter, the Shepherd of Hermas, the Epistle of Barnabas, and 1 and 2 Clement. A list that corresponds precisely with the 27 books of today's New Testament did not appear until the year 367 A.D. Even after this list—composed by Athanasius—many churches continued to use collections that varied widely. Think about it. There was no Bible as we know it until more than three hundred years after Jesus. That's a long time.

So how, then, did we ultimately get our Scripture in its final form? The conclusive event occurred sometime between 375-400 A.D. when a scholar named Jerome translated both the Old and New Testaments into Latin. Known as the Vulgate, this became the official Bible of the Roman Catholic Church. Jerome followed Athanasius's list of 27 New Testament books, and the rest is history. Thus, a number of writings once considered Scripture by many Christians have been all but totally forgotten today.

Furthermore, even at the present time different Christian traditions have different Bibles. The Catholic Bible, as you may be aware, is larger than the Protestant Bible—it has more books. Size matters. Up until Martin Luther and the Protestant Reformers in the 1,500s, the Christian Bible featured a much larger Old Testament, namely, those so-called Deuterocanonical books that you have been waiting to learn about—books such as Judith, Susanna, Tobit, and Bel and the Dragon, which, by the way, are really great stories. As part of their "protest" against the Catholic Church, the Reformers decided that those books should not be included. Thus many Protestant Christians have never even heard of books that were canonized prior to the 1,500s and remain in the Catholic Bible today.

Alright, maybe you are not impressed with Bel and the Dragon or which Christians have a bigger cannon. Perhaps these facts seem to be nothing more than interesting tidbits about the history of the Bible. But wait, there's more. On closer inspection, they actually raise some deep questions: If the process of writing was divinely inspired, was the process of canonization also guided by God? If not, then was it mere mortals who decided what should be in the Bible? And if yes, then when and where did divine inspiration cease—as soon as the list of books was set? What were the criteria for determining if a book made it or not? Who set the criteria? How are we to treat books that just missed the cut? Why don't we ever talk about them today? Shouldn't we at least be familiar with their content in order to be better informed about our faith tradition? What if we read them and found them every bit as meaningful and true as the books in the Bible? Moreover, what about the fact that Paul in his letters to the Corinthians refers to other letters, now lost, which he wrote to that church? Were these letters to the Corinthians inspired? Would they have been in the Bible if they had survived? If so, does that mean that we have lost part of God's word? Are there other lost books that should have been included? And speaking of losing God's word, were the Protestant Reformers wrongly tinkering with Scripture when they axed books from the Bible?

Well, that's a start anyway. Yes, it's quite intricate. Thus, it's much easier to act like the Bible that we know today — whatever Bible that may be — was handed to us by God. But it wasn't. It's got a lot of human fingerprints all over it, which leads to one final point.

Given that the formation of the Bible was a long process, the writers of the individual books presumably had little sense that they were writing Scripture. The various books were addressed to specific audiences in specific times and places; the authors did not know that their work would end up alongside 65 other books as Holy Writ. Accordingly, there is not one passage in the Bible that claims that the Bible is the inspired Word of God. How could it?

This is a fairly key fact that is rarely considered: The Bible does not declare any special or uniquely divine status for itself. Rather, it is the Christian tradition which pronounces that its chosen list of sacred books is the inspired Word of God. What about the oft-cited 2 Timothy 3:16: "All Scripture is inspired by God . . ."? Here "Scripture" refers only to the Old Testament, as that was the only Scripture which existed at the time. It could not refer to the Bible as a whole, since the New Testament canon had not been determined — some of the books had not even been written.

It would be sort of nice, wouldn't it, if the Bible — as the Koran does — declared itself to be the Word of God. You know, maybe some sort of post-script putting God's stamp of approval on the entire thing. Oh well.

DID YOU GET MY TEXT?

We have no original manuscripts of any biblical text. Not even close. What exists are copies of copies of copies. So what do we do when the existing manuscripts do not agree with one another? How do we decide which copy is closer to the original? That is, how do scholars decide which manuscript to translate? It can become very complicated very quickly, but the basic idea is easy enough to grasp.

Modern English translations of the Old Testament are based on Hebrew manuscripts — called the Masoretic Text — that date to about 1000 A.D. That is one thousand years ago, not one thousand years before Jesus. That means there is about 1,500 years between the writing of the originals and the manuscripts that we have. As one can imagine, errors have crept in, accidentally or intentionally. Many, though not all, of today's translations indicate with a footnote — those little letters next to words in your study Bible — where a textual problem exists and how the translators resolved it.

One way they solve it is to check the Septuagint, always a popular sermon topic. As time went by, fewer Jews could read the original Hebrew, so the Scripture was translated into Greek, the commonly spoken language of the day, around 150 B.C. When modern translators come to a difficult Hebrew text, they consult the Septuagint hoping that it provides some clues: perhaps the translators of the Septuagint were working with more accurate and reliable Hebrew manuscripts. Thus, by looking at their rendering, translators can figure out the original Hebrew that was behind it.

Sometimes, however, today's translators simply choose to render the Septuagint, even though the original Hebrew is perfectly clear. One example of this is Isaiah 7:14.

The Hebrew reads: "A young woman will conceive and bear a son." There is a different Hebrew word for "virgin" which is not used here. For some reason, however, the Septuagint translators rendered the Hebrew word for "young woman" with the Greek word for "virgin" instead of with the separate Greek word for "young woman." Remarkably, many modern translations of Isaiah 7:14 arbitrarily decide not to render the Hebrew and to follow the Greek instead. And it is easy to see why: Matthew 1:23 has also followed the Septuagint and applied it to Mary and Jesus: "Behold, a virgin will conceive and bear a son." So translators, motivated by a theological agenda — to advance the virgin birth of Jesus — elect to deviate from the clear Hebrew of Isaiah 7:14 and render the Greek instead.

In short, translators can decide to follow the Septuagint instead of the original Hebrew whenever they want for whatever reason they want — and they don't always tell us. Pretty sneaky of them, isn't it?

Textual critics can also consult other ancient translations of the Hebrew, such as the Syriac Peshitta (which gets the vulgar-sounding-name award), Latin Vulgate, and the Aramaic Targums. Google those if you want more information on those fascinating texts. The more in vogue Dead Sea Scrolls offer another option for translators. When these texts were found in 1947 near the ancient city of Qumran, they pushed back the dates of our earliest Hebrew manuscripts more than one thousand years. Composed by a group of Jews in Palestine about a century before Jesus, these scrolls feature many biblical and non biblical texts. While there is certainly no complete Old Testament among the Dead Sea documents, there are partial scrolls from every

Old Testament book except Esther, which saddens me personally, since she was such a good girl.

There are numerous differences between the Masoretic Text—remember, those are the ones from which we get our modern translations and they date to only one thousand years ago—and the Dead Sea Scrolls, though most of them are relatively minor. One good example of a more significant disparity is found at the end of 1 Samuel 10 where the Qumran text features a lengthy paragraph that provides essential background information for the story that follows in chapter eleven. One modern translation, the NRSV, includes the paragraph, which means that those translators decided that it was probably in the original Hebrew and was somehow lost in the copying process. Other modern translations do not include it. It's basically a guess and different translation committees guess differently. Indeed, you might just be surprised (or you may not care) at how often they deviate from the Hebrew and instead render the Greek of the Septuagint or the Dead Sea Scrolls, especially in certain books like Samuel and Hosea which are littered with textual problems.

The transmission of the New Testament is plagued with the same basic set of issues. Our modern day translations are based on manuscripts that date to about 300-400 A.D.—thus several hundred years after the originals. The most valuable manuscript is Codex Sinaiticus, which was not discovered until the mid-1800s in a monastery at the base of Mount Sinai—hence the name. In addition to the entire New Testament, Sinaiticus also includes the Epistle of Barnabas and the Shepherd of Hermas.

The other major manuscript is Codex Vaticanus. It, however, is missing part of the book of Hebrews, several of

Paul's letters, and Revelation. Notably, then, the two most important ancient manuscripts on which our current New Testament translations are based either contain two works that are totally unknown to most Christians or are missing several books.

Besides Sinaiticus and Vaticanus, scholars must consult a variety of translations made in Syriac, Coptic, Latin, and other languages, quotations from early church writers, and over five thousand manuscript copies of the New Testament. Now, I know what you are thinking (besides "I really need to learn Coptic"): Five thousand manuscripts?! But it's not that bad—or good, I guess—since virtually all of these five thousand feature only a small part of the New Testament—anywhere from a couple of books to a few words. And no two of them are exactly identical, which makes reconstructing the original New Testament text a major challenge.

Many of the differences among the manuscripts were probably caused by innocent mistakes in copying—when scribes got sleepy or sloppy or distracted by Monday Night Football. Some of the discrepancies, however, seem to result from intentional alterations that were motivated by theological concerns. When scribes rewrite the Word of God, purposefully changing the original to make it conform to their beliefs, the stakes get quite a bit higher. Here are just two examples:

Some of the oldest manuscripts, including Sinaiticus, do not contain the phrase "son of God" in Mark 1:1. It is possible that this phrase was inserted later to rebut a belief among some Christians that Jesus did not become God's son until his baptism. Likewise, in some early manuscripts of Luke 3:22, the voice from heaven at Jesus' baptism proclaims: "You are my son; *today* I have begotten you," which implies that Jesus does not become the "son of God" until his baptism. Most modern translations follow other manuscripts which avoid the theological question by saying, "with you I am well-pleased" or "in you I delight" instead of "*today* I have begotten you." This might seem somewhat trivial. But let's pause for a tick. Did the original New Testament manuscripts suggest that Jesus was not *born* as the son of God and only came to be so when he emerged from the baptismal waters? Is the belief that Jesus was born divine based on some bogus scribal editorializing? There is some serious, if nerdy, stuff going on here.

A second example occurs in several late manuscripts of 1 John 5:7-8, where a scribe inserted an explicit reference to the Trinity by adding the lengthy phrase: "The Father, the Word, and the Holy Spirit, and these three are one." Nearly all contemporary translations do not follow this reading, since the vast majority of 1 John manuscripts do not have this phrase. The couple of translations that do (e.g., the New King James) are clearly motivated by a theological agenda.

Finally, the ending of the Gospel of Mark is the biggest and best known textual issue in the whole Bible — I am sure you can't believe I waited this long to bring it up. The oldest manuscripts of Mark end at 16:8, which, according to most scholars, is original. But it's an uncomfortable conclusion: frightened women fleeing from the empty tomb of Jesus too afraid to speak to anyone. Other manuscripts add one more verse, the so-called "shorter ending of Mark" (a phrase which I don't like too well), which reports that Jesus himself appeared to the disciples. Some manuscripts then add, or replace the shorter ending with, the "longer ending of Mark" which features Jesus appearing to Mary Magdalene and to two disciples before commissioning all the disciples and ascending to heaven. Most modern translations include both the shorter and longer ending despite their not being present in the oldest manuscripts. Check to see how your Bible does it.

In sum, there is not one simple manuscript on which Bible translations are based; and we will never be able to reconstruct the original Hebrew and Greek texts. We can perhaps take some comfort in the fact that most of the variants do not significantly alter the meaning of the text. But that still leaves those that do. Scribes could rewrite the Bible to fit with their own beliefs. And they evidently did, though it's not always clear when and where, which is what makes this so potentially unsettling.

Further questions arise: Are only the originals inspired? If so, why would God inspire only the first copy of a text and then watch as it was erroneously transmitted by scribes, leaving us today with a flawed copy? If little errors have crept in, how do we know that there aren't larger ones as well? Who decides when to translate the Masoretic Text or Sinaiticus and when to deviate from it—and what authority do they have? Aren't translators making decisions for us about what's in the Bible? Isn't that a lot of power for one person or committee? Just like the ancient scribes, then, they too can make the text conform to their views by choosing certain manuscripts over others?

WHAT'S LOST IN TRANSLATION?

Most Christians cannot read the original Word of God. They can only read a translation of it. A translation is essentially an interpretation. A lot can be lost in the process.

Anyone who has studied a language other than their native one understands this principle. Imagine the difficulty of translating an ancient dead dialect into a modern language. Hence the variety among Bible translations — they are each different *interpretations* of the original. Most of us, then, are utterly at the mercy of the translator. We already knew that, I suppose. But still, we should ponder its significance for a moment. If we cannot read the original Hebrew or Greek, we cannot read the Word of God. Period. God does not speak English. We must depend on someone, or, more likely, some committee, who can translate it for us. Pick any verse from the Bible — even the shortest one, John 11:35 — and you will find different renderings.

Sometimes those differences are minor; in other cases there are serious implications. To take but one example, the translation of Philippians 2:6 hinges on the interpretation of one Greek verb, which yields various theological meanings about the relationship between God and Jesus. The King James offers a translation that is consistent with the traditional belief that Jesus is the second person of the Trinity: "Let this mind be in you, which was also in Christ Jesus: Who, being in the form of God, thought it not robbery to be equal with God." Here Jesus is "equal" with God. Most modern versions, however, render it more ambiguously: "though he was in the form of God, did not regard equality with God as something to be exploited" (NRSV) or "did not consider equality with God as something to be grasped" (NIV). Here it's not clear whether or not Jesus has equality with God. One verb, different implications for understanding the Trinity — and yet another reason to spend two years learning Greek.

Think about how often we miscommunicate with one another — even when one person is not watching TV. We are speaking verbally, face-to-face in the same language, with facial expressions and intonation to assist us, and we still misunderstand (unless perhaps it was during a commercial). It's easy to see, then, how potentially hazardous it is to take written Hebrew and Greek texts composed by people centuries ago who wore tunics, had no electricity, and did not know that North America even existed, and to translate it into contemporary English for people with cell phones and automobiles. It's a long, long bridge that translators are trying to build. And our only option — unless we know the original language and can build our own — is to walk across those bridges. If nothing else, we should at least acknowledge how much faith we place in translations every time we read Scripture.

Yeah, the Tower of Babel really messed things up for us.

WHAT DO YOU SAY?

Now it's your turn.

Scholars first decide which manuscript to render; then they must determine how to translate it into English. Both of those are difficult tasks fraught with subjective interpretation. But a third and final one is even trickier, and the job is left up to us: how we interpret the words that we read. Textual critics and translators can do their thing, but if you and I do not read the Bible, it remains nothing more than words on a page. It has no meaning until someone reads it.

To illustrate this point with my students I sometimes open up the Bible, lay it on the desk, and announce that we will now let the Bible speak to us. I stand there, listening intently for a few moments, head tilted, hand cupped around my ear. Listening. Listening. Of course there is only silence. This is the point at which students start to think I am not playing with a full deck. But my trump card is simple: The Bible only speaks — it only "means" something — when people read it.

Meaning, then, arises at the intersection between a biblical text and a reader. And readers are different. They have different ages, races, genders, levels of intelligence, life experiences, geographic locations, socio-economic positions, political views, religious backgrounds, and wireless providers. All of these variables come into play when people read the Bible. We don't expect a ten-year-old to interpret the Scripture like a thirty-year-old; an affluent American like an impoverished Haitian; a highly educated woman like a male high school dropout; a rabbi like a priest. And they don't. When a person reads the Bible, everything about who they are at that moment influences how they interpret it. That is true for everybody. And since it takes a person and a text to make meaning, there are many different, legitimate, perfectly good interpretations of a single biblical text. (If you are thinking that God wrote the Bible and we can pray and ask God to reveal the one, single, correct meaning, that's fine. But then, with all due respect, you will have to explain how so many different people pray and come up with radically disparate ideas.)

Let's take it a step further. Since we cannot interview the authors of the Bible, we will never know whether or not our interpretations are in line with what was intended. But even if we could ask them exactly what they meant, would that mean that there was only one right interpretation? Imagine having a conversation with a modern poet or novelist about their work in which we offered some interpretations that they did not necessarily intend. Would that make our thoughts wrong? Would the author emphatically deny the legitimacy of our perspective? Maybe. But more than likely, the author would be engaged by our insights as we brought new levels of meaning to their work. Once a text is written, it takes on a life of its own independent from the author who cannot control how it is construed. The same presumably would be true of biblical authors: they would be thrilled — if not shocked — that their work continues to be read and discussed, that their writing is still alive, even if it were being understood in ways that did not conform to the specific original intention.

In brief, preachers pretend that we can determine definitively the single, right reading of a biblical passage. The raw truth is that we cannot. So perhaps the best approach is to embrace the diversity of interpretations and learn from others. If you are an American, try reading Psalm 23 with an African shepherd. If you are wealthy, read the story of the Exodus with a peasant from Guatemala. If you are a "conservative," try reading Matthew 25 with a "liberal." If you are healthy, read the stories of Jesus' healing miracles with someone dying of cancer. If you cannot find these people, check the internet — people write stuff about the Bible there. If you don't know what you are, heck, just read with anybody. You will likely see the text in ways you never imagined. And that is a good thing. But it also means there are different valid interpretations. And that can be a hard thing.

This may be a good time to remind you of the obvious. I'll feel better about myself if I do. I, just like pastors and everybody else, interpret the Bible. As a human subject, it is impossible for me to provide a truly objective reading. While I am doing my best to let Scripture speak for itself, I recognize that cannot truly happen. My approach to and reading of Scripture is shaped by numerous factors, some of which I am probably not even aware. It's necessary for us to admit the subjectivity of our own interpretations — particularly for those of us who write books and deliver sermons. We have certain inherent, inescapable biases and agendas. Not in a bad sense, just in an inevitable human sense. Unfortunately, not everyone attempts to make theirs transparent, to come clean, which can become problematic. So, again, for the record, here is my agenda — at least so far as I am aware: I want Christians to read and ruminate carefully about the Bible, the whole Bible, for themselves. And then to discuss what they read and think with others.

ARE WE DIGGING FOR TRUTH?

If your faith rests on archeology corroborating the Bible, your faith lies in ruins. Despite what you might have seen on TV or heard at a church conference, archaeology does not prove the Bible true. Or false. It does not verify its reliability. Or inaccuracy. Archeology is not about faith. Archaeology studies past human cultures by examining their material remains, including buildings, tools, artwork, and documents. It has nothing to do with religious truth claims.

Archaeologists dig up artifacts that can provide background information by filling out the social and cultural context for the biblical stories. Sometimes they seem to fit together fairly well. For example, archaeologists have found evidence that the camel was domesticated in the

Middle East by the eighteenth century B.C. — which was great since as everyone knows, wild camels are a real nuisance. Thus, when Genesis portrays Abraham traveling with camels, it fits the historical context. Likewise, Egyptian records of domestic slaves include a couple of names found in the Bible — not the same people, just the same names, like "Bob." Egyptian writings also feature the term "hapiru" which many scholars believe is closely related to the term "Hebrew." The Merneptah Inscription, dating to about 1210 B.C., mentions that a people called Israel inhabited the land of Canaan. While these are important discoveries, they only provide a general context or framework for the Old Testament narratives; they do not prove that the stories really happened.

How about we try this. Let's say that five hundred years from now, archaeologists find the then-ancient ruins of New York City when they uncover dilapidated skyscrapers and subways. Would that mean that the *Great Gatsby* — a fictional story set in New York City — really happened, that it was accurate history? Obviously not. Simply because future archaeologists unearthed evidence that New York City existed does not in any way make it probable that the *Great Gatsby* actually occurred. Likewise, just because the Bible mentions the ancient Egyptian city of Ramses does not mean that the story of the Exodus is historically accurate.

Here's another thought experiment. Let's say that three thousand years hence, many Christians believe that God punished the then-ancient city of New Orleans by wiping it out with a massive hurricane in the early 2000s. Say, then, that sure enough, archaeologists excavating the Gulf Coast discover evidence of major water and wind damage to the city of New Orleans dated to about that time. Would that prove the theological belief that God destroyed the city? Clearly not. Archeology and theology are two totally different games. Likewise, if archaeologists found that the city of Jericho suffered a sudden and violent collapse, would that prove that the Israelites marched around the city seven times, blew their trumpets, and watched as God miraculously collapsed the walls, as Joshua 6 says? Again, no. Archaeology cannot validate the Bible's claim of divine intervention.

But let's back up and forget theology for a moment. Archaeology is very, very far from confirming the historical accuracy of the Bible—farther than Tunisia from winning the winter Olympics. We have nothing tangible whatsoever to suggest that Abraham, Isaac, Jacob, Joseph, Moses, Joshua, Samson, and Samuel ever even existed. David is the first character for whom we have some data—but just that he was a real person, not that he had sex with Bathsheba. There is, then, no archaeological evidence to support major Old Testament events, which could easily be substantiated by sources outside the Bible.

For instance, it is virtually inconceivable that the ten plagues of Moses could have occurred as told in the Bible without leaving at least some physical evidence. If the first born of every household in Egypt had died on a single night (the tenth plague; Exodus 12:29-30), that would have been the watershed event in Egyptian history. Imagine how the entire Egyptian culture and civilization would have been irreversibly altered in one stroke. Yet there is not a single word about it in any of the numerous existing Egyptian writings—nothing in official court records, no poem of lament, no evidence of mass burials, nothing. The same thing can be said for the devastation of the Egyptian army in the Red Sea (Exodus 13:28), or how 600,000 Israelite men (Exodus 12:37), not counting women, children, and their possessions (and women don't pack lightly), could have exited Egypt at one time. It would have taken at least a week for that many people to cross the Red Sea, and that's only if no one stopped to snap pictures. There is simply no evidence for any of it.

Likewise, according to Joshua 10-12, the Israelites invaded and completely demolished numerous cities in Canaan. If this were historically accurate, it is unimaginable that there would not be copious physical and documented evidence supporting it. But there isn't.

Now the lack of evidence does not "prove" that these stories did not happen. After all, anything is possible. I could claim that there are three beach balls revolving around Saturn right now. Just because there is no physical evidence to prove that the balls exist does not rule out the possibility that my claim is true. But the burden of proof would be on me to demonstrate the veracity of my assertion, not on you to "prove" that the beach balls don't exist. The same is true for the Bible. If you claim that the ten plagues and crossing of the Red Sea really happened, then the burden of proof is on you. So far no proof exists. Christians should understand that.

Archaeology and the Bible can be a dirty topic. Sometimes you have to dig deeper to get to the truth.

IS THE BIBLE PLAGIARIZED?

The Bible is not unique. It is very similar to many other ancient writings in its form, style, content, and theology. This is nothing against the Bible, but it does mean that we will probably see Scripture in a different light after reading Egyptian, Canaanite, Babylonian, and Greco-Roman works which could easily pass for the Bible if only the names were changed.

Before we run through a series of examples, it should be made clear that dating ancient manuscripts can be very difficult — though probably not as difficult as dating a teenage guy or girl. It's very hard to determine the precise time when ancient manuscripts were written and assessing the length of the oral tradition behind them is impossible. Thus, we cannot say with any degree of certainty if the biblical writers copied ideas from other ancient texts, or if the reverse is true. Or if they just happened to come up with some of the same stuff independently. But regardless, the point is that the Bible did not drop from heaven void of any connections to the world around it; rather, Scripture is quite at home in its cultural, historical, and literary context. In many ways, the Bible is a collection of common writings from the ancient Middle East.

Exhibit A: There are a number of ancient flood stories outside of the biblical tradition. Perhaps the best known one is in the Gilgamesh Epic. In this account, the Babylonian deities instruct a man named Utnapishtim — probably called U-Nap by his friends — to construct a large boat in order to survive the flood that they are about to unleash. Utnapishtim complies, takes on board his family and animals, and rides out the deluge. The ship comes to rest on a mountain; Utnapishtim sends out birds to determine if it's safe to exit; he then offers sacrifices; the gods enjoy the smell (cf. Genesis 8:20-21) and promise never to forget this catastrophe. This basic story line is amazingly similar to the biblical one.

Exhibit B: The well-known story of the birth of Moses in Exodus 2:1-10 — remember the baby in a basket in the Nile — is almost identical to the account of the birth of Sargon, an ancient king of Akkad (Babylon). Sargon tells us that his mother, a high priestess, gave birth to him secretly — though he does not say why. His mother put him in a reed basket, sealing it with tar. She placed the basket in a river where it floated downstream until someone found him and raised him as his adopted son. As Sargon grew up, Ishtar, a goddess, blessed him, enabling him to become a great king.

Exhibit C: The Old Testament laws are similar in many respects to the Law Code of Hammurabi. In this instance, it is certain that the Code of Hammurabi is older. He was a Babylonian king who ruled from c. 1795-1750 B.C. Hammurabi, like the biblical text, claimed that his laws were revealed to him by the deity, specifically Shamash, the god of justice. Here are a couple of the many parallels: Mosaic Law demands in Exodus 21:23-25 that "you are to take life for life, eye for eye, hand for hand, foot for foot, burn for burn, wound for wound, stripe for stripe." Hammurabi declares, "If a man puts out the eye of another man, his eye shall be put out. If he breaks another man's bone, his bone shall be broken. If a man knocks out the teeth of his equal, his teeth shall be knocked out."

Moses and Hammurabi both had laws concerning children who struck their parents. In the Bible, the penalty for the child is death (Exodus 21:15). Hammurabi let the offender off easy, requiring only that their hands be cut off. Hammurabi outlawed adultery, as well as intercourse between a father and daughter, son and mother, or father and daughter-in-law. The penalty was usually death. Leviticus 18 has a similar list of prohibited sexual relations. (See, weird sex has been going on for centuries.) Both law codes permitted a man to divorce his wife if she displeased him. Hammurabi, however, required that the husband provide his ex-wife with a certain fraction of his money and property on which to live and raise the children. Mosaic Law imposed no such requirement on the man (Deuteronomy 24:1).

In Hammurabi's law, if a man sold himself and his family to compensate for a debt, they were to labor for three years, but in the fourth year the family was to be set free. Mosaic Law stated that if an Israelite worked as a servant to pay off a debt, he would serve six years and in the seventh year be released (Exodus 21:2). Neither code permitted filing for chapter eleven bankruptcy.

Exhibit D: The Mesha Inscription is particularly fascinating since it is a non-Israelite text which mentions a biblical figure. King Mesha of Moab records how Omri King of Israel oppressed him for many days (1 Kings 16) because Chemosh, the Moabite god, was angry. Chemosh, who appears in the Bible (Judges 11:24 and elsewhere), deals with his people the Moabites in much the same way that the Lord handles the Israelites, punishing them with oppression when they displease him. When the Moabites are victorious, credit goes to Chemosh, just as the Israelites praise the Lord their God. When King Mesha attacks Israel, he slaughters every person in honor of Chemosh, which is strikingly reminiscent of the Israelites doing the same thing to fulfill the Lord's command (Joshua 6; 10:28-42).

Exhibit E: Singing songs of praise to your God—or god or gods or goddesses—is a universal religious phenomenon. Thus, we find many connections between the book of Psalms and other ancient literature. One case is the similarity between Psalm 104 and the Egyptian Hymn to Aten, written about 1400 B.C. Both hymns are a celebration of the deity as creator. Here are some of the specifics: Both songs (a) begin with the mention of light; (b) sing of the beauty of water flowing down the mountains; (c) speak generally of beasts, birds, fish, plants, and trees; (d) praise the deity for sustaining their creation; (e) mention lions in association with darkness; and (f) proclaim the wonders of creation and the god who created it. Indeed, the Hymn to Aten is indistinguishable from many of the biblical psalms, which I proved one day when I gave a copy of it to my students and told them it was from the Bible. I revealed the truth after about 15 minutes of discussion. Some of them seemed a little annoyed, but I think deep down they thought it was pretty cool.

Exhibit F: Nearly all cultures have wise guys. So it is not surprising that the book of Proverbs can be compared to many other texts, both ancient and modern. One association is particularly compelling. The Instructions of Amenemopet—who should have instructed his mother to give him a more pronounceable name—is an ancient Egyptian work containing thirty chapters of wise sayings. It mirrors Proverbs 22:17-23:11 in a number of ways, perhaps the most interesting of which is Proverbs 22:20 which says, "Have I not written for you thirty sayings of admonition . . ." In addition to the typical pieces of advice that appear in both works—listen carefully, obey your elders, don't make friends with a hothead—there are a few unusual similarities such as Amenemopet's, "Do not carry off the landmark at the boundaries of the arable land, nor encroach upon the boundaries of a widow" and Proverbs', "Do not remove an ancient landmark or encroach on the fields of orphans."

Exhibit G: Specific textual parallels to the New Testament are of a different nature. There were a plethora of Greek and Roman religions in the Middle East about the time that Christianity was developing. But exactly what they believed is difficult to determine since a number of them were "mystery religions" and thus intentionally secretive. Here's what we do know.

In general, many Christian tenets are similar to those of other ancient Mediterranean religions. Mythologies featured stories of miraculous births, perhaps even virginal conceptions. Thus, "Son of God" language was not uncommon. Certain traditions told of wandering teachers and miracle workers who had a band of disciples. They also had water rituals akin to baptism and communal meals not unlike the Eucharist. We also find the association of spilled blood and salvation. The idea of gaining eternal life (immortality) runs through a number of ancient religions, as does the belief that the underworld contained fiery rivers and lakes which threatened sinners. Furthermore, scholars have devoted a fair bit of attention to stories about "dying and rising" gods. None of them are identical to the story of Jesus, but it is clear that several ancient mythological figures perish and return to life in some fashion.

If the Bible must be unique to be true, then it's not true. But it is a logical fallacy to assert that for something to be true, it must be completely unlike anything else. The simple fact is that the Bible and many features of Christianity resemble other ancient texts and religions. Our basic ideas are not unique; and that is worth knowing. This fact does not compromise or indict our tradition, but it does mean we have more to contemplate.

RAW REFLECTIONS

So what do we do with these facts? How can we digest them? As always, each of us must answer that question for ourselves. There are no simple solutions that will appeal to all Christians. But, and here's the super-short indispensable conclusion, Christians, at the very least, need to be aware of these details, even if they don't become experts in them. We don't each need to learn Hebrew and Greek. But we should know that the Bible was not written in English and understand the implications that flow from that. We don't need to subscribe to *Biblical Archaeology Review* (yes, that's a real magazine, right behind *People* on the top seller list), but we should know what archaeologists have found and how their work relates to our faith. And the list goes on.

For me, and the dispensable reflections, the raw facts point to the human element in the Bible and our tradition. God is present, but God is not alone. People, with their faults, biases, and limited perspectives, are right there alongside God in the making and sustaining of our tradition. God could have dropped a book to earth, complete with everything we wanted and needed to know. But God didn't. Instead, God works with human messiness — the messiness of the specific historical and cultural location into which the Scripture came, the messiness of its formation, transmission, translation, and interpretation. The preposition here is important: God works "with" human beings, not "through" human beings. It's not a matter of God "using" humans to convey truth, as if humans are some passive vehicle through which God works. Rather, God is working alongside, "with," humans in the process.

This idea dovetails nicely with belief in the Incarnation of God in the person of Jesus. God was made manifest in a human being, so shouldn't we expect God to continue working with human beings. Scripture is "God-breathed" — breathed by the complex God whom we met earlier, in which case it would only make sense for our Scripture and tradition to be a bit chaotic and untidy. After all, Jesus, as we also saw earlier, was no easy Incarnation.

The human fingerprints in our faith are also evident in other world religions, both past and present. If God works with humans, it is difficult for me to see how any one religion, including our own, can claim to have captured all truth. There are too many people who have lived on this planet to think that God chose only one time, place, and religion to make the single, final revelation. The very facts that we encountered in this final course — such as the process by which the Bible was formed, and the process of interpretation that keeps Scripture alive — point to the ongoing nature of revelation, that it is not confined to one event or person. It is a process, over time, requiring different people. God has worked with humans in different times and places within our tradition; thus it is only natural to postulate that God works in many other ways, and times, and places, with other people. If this is the case, then we as Christians should adopt an attitude of sincere openness toward those of different faiths. Perhaps they too are part of the process of divine revelation.

But again, these are merely my raw reflections. The main thing is that we face the unfiltered, unprocessed facts about our Scripture and the history of our tradition. Good books, friends, pastors, and prayer may help us in the digestion process. But it's a process we should undertake as we seek to grow in wisdom and in favor with God, just as Jesus himself did (Luke 2:52).

Final Suggestions

Christians need God's raw Revelation to nourish and sustain us. We need its pure power. The unadulterated, all natural Scripture is better for us than the church's cooked version. But raw Revelation is hard — hard to swallow, even harder to digest. The preacher's platter, by contrast, is attractive and delicious. But there is a price to pay. A steady diet of a candy-coated, jelly-filled Scripture has made us spiritually overweight diabetics. A lazy and sedentary religious life is no way to honor our Maker.

It's time to change our habits. It's time to get off the couch of half-truths and easy answers and start the grueling but rewarding work of loving God with our minds. It will be difficult since our palates and bodies are so accustomed — addicted — to the sweetened Bible. It will take persistence to acquire a taste for the raw Scripture, to adjust to the assiduous work required for a vibrant, robust faith. Yes, it may be unpleasant at first. But ultimately our faith will be much stronger. And that is what matters.

Let me suggest five steps that we might take in order to accomplish this objective. As you might imagine, I loathe the idea that we can reduce things to simple formulas and programs. Four steps to intimacy with God. Five tricks for a happy marriage. Life's not that easy. We know that. Nonetheless, it might be helpful to structure our final thoughts in terms of concrete recommendations for Christians who desire a life of sacred vitality fueled by the unexpurgated Word of God.

Step 1: Pray. Meditate. Begin the meal by thanking God for the food and asking that it nourish your heart, soul, and mind. Ask God to help you deal honestly with God's Word. Ask for courage. Pray that you will be open to the new and unexpected, the exciting and terrifying. Pray that God will give you the strength to confront the challenges and difficulties that may arise. Ask for boldness and confidence. Commune with God.

When we spend time in God's Word, we are invigorated and refreshed and we come to know God more intimately. When we stop reading and thinking, we stop loving God. When we stop arguing, we stop caring. Where there is no struggle, there is no relationship. Therefore, do not conform to the easy religiosity of this world which requires no effort on your part, but rather be transformed by the renewing of your mind so that you can better love God with it (yes, that's an expanded version of Romans 12:2).

Step 2: Use your brain. Realize that God gave you a mind so that you can engage his Word. The fact that we have the power to reason suggests that God welcomes the queries and even the protests. If God did not want us to think, he would not have given us that ability. Embrace the idea that God wishes for us to partake of his Revelation in its original, unprocessed form.

The Bible is the Word of God in human language, which implies that we can only relate to God through our humanness, the most fundamental aspect of which is our intellect. We cannot fear the questions which may emerge. The only thing we have to fear is fear itself—as I think somebody famous once said. The Bible is a book which demands that we ask questions, so we cannot be afraid that God will disapprove of the ruminating and reasoning that his Word requires of us. What we should fear is swallowing whole what preachers try to spoon feed us. We cannot believe something merely because it has been repeated over and over, for years and years, by clergy and others in positions of authority. No, we must learn that the unanswered questions aren't nearly as dangerous as the unquestioned answers.

God gave us a brain as a tool to search for truth. He didn't give it to us so that we could be brain washed into worshipping false idols set up by human beings. Failing to analyze and interrogate is to deny our being made in the image and likeness of God, the greatest Mind of all.

It is tyrants and dictators, not God, who want people to be mindless followers. The truth has no fear of inquiry. Thus, boldly pursue truth no matter where it leads. No matter where. No . . . matter . . . where.

To that end, every sentence I have written in this book should be understood not as an assertion, but as a question.

Step 3: Commit to reading the Bible regularly. Develop a specific schedule. Be consistent; be diligent. Do not be lazy. God doesn't approve of spiritual lassitude.

Read through whole books in one sitting if possible, rather than from a chapter here and a chapter there. Read interactively, which is what the very nature and shape of the Bible asks of us. The Bible does not tell us directly what to think, what to do, or how to live. Rather, the truth comes indirectly through stories, poetry, songs, and letters; not didactic monologue. Thus we must engage the Scripture in conversation. We must treat it as a good friend who has many interesting things to say about love, forgiveness, jealousy, justice, deception, hope, fear, failure, and other areas of our lives. Indeed, there are numerous riveting biblical texts that we have not sampled, and which you are not likely to get in church either. We might not always like what the Bible says, but that's fine. We don't like everything our friends say or do either, but they remain our friends. The Bible is like a close companion who extends our imaginations as we contemplate life's philosophical, theological, ethical, and existential questions. In the process it awakens us to new modes of being and thinking, fresh ways of experiencing and viewing the world.

The Scripture draws us in with its rich and complex narratives, characters, and themes; its many fissures, ambiguities, and multiple levels of meaning beckon us. Thus, as you read, pose questions. Probe. Explore. Make note of what the text does not say — its gaps and silences. Consider what other biblical passages come to mind. Ask yourself how different people might interpret it. Interrupt the text with your own ideas. Assess the ethics and values endorsed by the text and whether you should condone or reject them. Read for enjoyment; read to be inspired and moved; read to be shaken to your very core.

The hard work of wrestling with the Word of God, as Abraham and others do, facilitates the growth of an authentic life of faith. Don't forget that the very name Israel means to contend with God. You may never know who you are until you have the self-discipline and fortitude to argue with God and God's raw Revelation.

Have a faith that is alive. Things that are alive can change.

Love God. Real love is vulnerable and hurts sometimes.

Step 4: Read with other people. Form a Bible book club, a community of readers, ideally one with some diversity. Exchange ideas with them; listen carefully to their perspectives and insights. Seek out different interpretations. Learn from what you read and from those with whom you talk. But also analyze their point of view: Why are they saying what they are saying? What's their agenda? Include your preacher and other church leaders as part of your cohort. Ask them the hard queries. Dialogue with them. Always examine matters for yourself. If, for example, you agree with everything I've said in this book, you're probably not scrutinizing carefully enough. If you disagree with everything, you probably have a preconceived platform. Be open. But be suspicious of all interpretations, including your own.

The raw Bible is not only better for us individually, but also communally. The process of open-minded thinking and reasoning with others helps to develop meaningful bonds with them. The Bible's complexity, its inclusion of multiple points of view, nurtures an acceptance of the tentative nature of knowledge, which in turn creates space for communication. Those who are willing to consider diverse perspectives — those who do not "know for sure" — are more open to dialogue. Listening to others is the first step toward loving them.

Some of us have been taught from an early age, per the Sunday school song, that we must "stand alone on the Word of God, the B-i-b-l-e." I never knew if "alone" meant "by yourself" or "not on any other book." Both are misguided. We should stand with others (not alone) and we should be willing to ponder what other books (not only the Bible) have to say about theological, spiritual, moral, and ethical topics. The Bible is not a book on which to stand. It's a book with which to sit. It's not a static, inert object. It's a living subject.

As you converse, try your best to be objective. That's essential. Remember the parable that Nathan told King David after David's sin with Bathsheba? It was a story about a rich man who greedily and selfishly took a poor man's only sheep. The story was an allegory—David himself was the rich man (let's overlook that Bathsheba is represented by an animal). David, however, did not realize this initially, so he pronounced punishment for the rich man. Then it dawned on David: he was the rich man. Nathan understood that sometimes humans see a situation quite differently when they see it more objectively. Nathan's story jolted David to recognize the truth. Perhaps the ultimate act of faith is to apply that same approach when dealing with the Bible itself, namely, to evaluate it rationally and impartially. Seeing ourselves and our Scripture as others do will set the table for real conversation, for the possibility of change, for finding the truth, just as it did for David.

If you read and contemplate and talk with others and end up with more questions than answers, that's fine. Keep going. It's about the journey more than the destination.

Step 5: Become a better human being. Be intentional about growing into a kinder person as a consequence of your encounter with the uncensored Word. Be self-conscious about allowing the complexity and ambiguity of Scripture to prepare you to handle with care and compassion your relationships with other complex people and to navigate the ambiguity of human existence. Ensure that your experience with the messiness of the unprocessed Bible empowers you to deal more faithfully with the messiness of real life. Become a more ethically and morally sensitive human being as a result of consuming the raw Revelation.

When we recognize that the Bible does not offer straightforward solutions to our questions, it helps us grapple with the idea that no one single person will either—whether a parent, politician, pastor, or philosopher. Nor will one ideology or one system or anything else. Life is too big for simple answers. When we embrace the idea that the Bible is not a book of black and white, it's easier to cope with the fact that life isn't either. This, in turn, makes us less dogmatic, more willing to hear different sides of the story. It makes us less judgmental. The more you know and understand the real Bible, the more you realize how little you know, which cultivates a genuine sense of humility and openness to others.

But we can be humble without being weak; we can be open without letting our brains fall out. Wrestling with Scripture makes us stronger and sharper mentally. The same critical capacities that we must exercise in handling the Bible can be applied to various arenas of our life—political, cultural, economic, and so on. Striving with the Word helps us to become savvy citizens of this earth and of the kingdom of God.

So that's it. Five easy steps and you are done.

Now let's end simply where we began. Read the Bible for yourself and think carefully about it. When we have the courage to partake of God's wonderfully raw Revelation we may experience a dynamic personal and communal transformation. The uncensored Bible is an invaluable, God-given resource for renewing ourselves, each other, and the world in which we live.

FURTHER READING

There are countless books (and blogs) that you might consider in your continued exploration of the Bible. Here are a few them.

Karen Armstrong, *The Bible: A Biography* (Grove, 2008).

Timothy Beal, *The Rise and Fall of the Bible* (Houghton Mifflin, 2011).

F. F. Bruce, *Hard Sayings of Jesus* (IVP, 1983).

Walter Brueggemann, *Theology of the Old Testament* (Fortress, 2005).

Michael Coogan, *A Brief Introduction to the Old Testament* (Oxford, 2008).

Bart Ehrman, *Misquoting Jesus* (HarperOne, 2007).

Gordon Fee and Douglas Stuart, *How To Read the Bible for All Its Worth* (Zondervan, 2003).

Richard Elliott Friedman, *Who Wrote the Bible?* (HarperOne 1987).

Christian Hauer and William Young, *Introduction to the Bible* (Pearson, 2011).

Luke Timothy Johnson, *The Writings of the New Testament* (Fortress, 2010).

Scot McKnight, *The Blue Parakeet* (Zondervan, 2010).

Victor Matthews, *Old Testament Parallels* (Paulist, 2007).

Jack Miles, *God: A Biography* (Vintage, 1996).

David Plotz, *Good Book* (Harper, 2009).

Susanne Scholz, *Biblical Studies Alternatively* (Pearson, 2002).

John Shelby Spong, *Rescuing the Bible from Fundamentalism* (HarperOne, 1992).

Lee Strobel, *The Case for Christ* (Zondervan, 1998).

Kristin Swenson, *Bible Babel* (Harper Perennial, 2011).

Walter Kaiser, et. al., *Hard Sayings of the Bible* (IVP, 1996).

22183872R00133

Made in the USA
Columbia, SC
27 July 2018